COMPLETE POEMS

KARIN BOYE
photograph by Atelier Jaeger

# KARIN BOYE

COMPLETE POEMS

TRANSLATED BY
David McDuff

BLOODAXE BOOKS

Translation © David McDuff 1994

ISBN: 978 1 85224 109 4

First published 1994 by
Bloodaxe Books Ltd,
Eastburn,
South Park,
Hexham,
Northumberland NE46 1BS.

www.bloodaxebooks.com
For further information about Bloodaxe titles
please visit our website or write to
the above address for a catalogue.

LEGAL NOTICE

All rights reserved. No part of this book may be
reproduced, stored in a retrieval system, or
transmitted in any form, or by any means, electronic,
mechanical, photocopying, recording or otherwise,
without prior written permission from Bloodaxe Books Ltd.

Requests to publish work from this book
must be sent to Bloodaxe Books Ltd.

David McDuff has asserted his right under
Section 77 of the Copyright, Designs and Patents Act 1988
to be identified as the author of this translation.

ACKNOWLEDGEMENTS

Acknowledgements are due to Arts Council England
for providing a translation grant for this book, and to
Kungl. Bibliotecket, Stockholm, for help with photographs.
The Swedish text used for this translation is Karin Boye's
Dikter (Bonniers, Stockholm, 1942), as reprinted in 1990.

Digital reprint of the 1994 Bloodaxe edition.

Contents

11   *Karin Boye: A Biographical Profile* by DAVID McDUFF

Clouds (1922)
34   Clouds
34   A Buddhist Fantasy
35   The Nightjar
36   To a Sphinx
37   Idea
37   Evening Prayer
38   Crossroads
39   The Best
39   Morning Song
40   Early Spring
41   A Painter's Wish
41   To an Unknown Descendant
42   Inwards
42   Bare Frost
43   The Spring's Expectancy
43   Wish-Night
44   O a blade…
45   You
45   Morning
46   Dream
47   To Beauty
47   Memory
48   The Exhortation
48   Recovery
49   The Doors
50   Homeless
50   If this life is the only one…
51   Small Things
51   Saved
51   Awakening
52   Explanation
52   You Are My Purest Consolation
53   The Maple
53   Dream Vision
54   The Gods
54   To Carolina Rediva

55	Anxiety
56	Via Media
56	Winter Night
57	Spellbound
57	The Nameless
58	Pray for One Thing

Hidden Lands (1924)

60	Elemental Spirits
61	The Thorn
61	Summer Day
62	The Way Home
62	To the Sea
63	Guiding Principle
63	The Stars
64	The Unknown One
64	Happy He That Has Gods
65	To a Poet
65	The Great Multitude
66	Learn To Be Silent
66	The Invisible Things
67	To Sleep
68	New Ways
68	Unscathed
69	Spring Song
70	The Stars' Solace
71	Evening Stillness
71	Victory
72	The Child
72	The Spring Water
73	You Shall Thank
73	Grandfather
74	Some Hearts Are Treasures
75	Tonight the Heaven Has No Garb
75	The Wanderer
76	Wish
77	To a Friend
78	Burning Candles
78	Songs About Fate
80	Æsir and Elves
83	The Tree
84	The Shield-Maiden

The Hearths (1927)

- 86   The Hearths
- 94   I Distrust...
- 95   In the Dark
- 95   Compelled
- 96   To the Shadow of a Reality
- 97   The Two Lineages
- 98   The Swallows
- 98   To Someone Who Is Very Young
- 99   I Want to Meet...
- 99   From a Bad Girl
- 100 The stars grow in the spring...
- 100 Torkel Tyre
- 102 The Carillon
- 103 The Condemned
- 104 The Man Without Mercy
- 105 Samson sings as he grasps the pillars of the temple
- 105 The Star
- 106 The Grass's Song
- 107 The Sea
- 108 On the Move
- 108 Of Those Who Fell Too Soon
- 109 The Falling Morning Star
- 110 The world is dreamt...
- 110 The World's Heart
- 111 The Corrupter
- 111 The Stones
- 112 We Sleepy Children
- 112 The Bygone Days
- 113 The Water Babies
- 113 Lilith's Song

For the Tree's Sake (1935)

- 116 Nowhere
- 116 Walpurgis Night
- 117 You Call for People
- 117 Cherub
- 118 That Hour
- 118 The Night's Deep Violoncello
- 119 Yes, of course it hurts
- 120 A Stillness Expanded
- 120 You Are the Seed

121	If I Could Follow You
121	Blonde Morning
122	Ripe as a Fruit
122	Farewell
123	Now I Know
123	My Skin Is Full of Butterflies
124	The Tree Beneath the Earth
125	Our Eyes Are Our Fate
126	Confession
127	Prayer to the Sun
127	Young Wills Whine
128	The Doorway
129	Idyll
130	For the Hour of Great Humiliation
130	Pyre
131	Invulnerable
131	Knowledge
132	Dwarf Pine
132	The Mouths
134	Sea Prayer
135	The Way Is Narrow
136	The Wanderer in the Desert
137	Your Warmth
137	Legend
140	Eternity
142	Fragment of Alcman

The Seven Deadly Sins and Other Posthumous Poems (1941)

144	The Seven Deadly Sins
156	A Form Am I
156	Odysseus at the Mast
158	Be Silent. Have Trust
159	The Trees
160	How Can Reliance Live?
161	Christmas 1939
162	Man's Multiplicity
163	We Who Do Not Dare to See
164	The Avenging Angel Speaks
165	They Stole Your Thought from You
165	Drinking Sacrifice
166	Marsh Wanderer
166	The Flower Bitterness

167	Never is the forest happy as now
167	Wild Apple
168	Now is the time of immense waiting
169	How can I say...
169	To You
169	My poor young thing...
170	You are the resurrection of my soul
171	Many voices speak
172	Your voice...
173	All things you contain...
173	Linköping Cathedral
176	Prologue at a School Prizegiving
177	Save the Children
178	The Child
180	Those Quiet Footsteps Behind Me
181	At the Bottom of Things
181	Where the divining-rod descends
182	Thus are we driven...
183	Those dark angels...
184	After Death

Two portraits of Karin Boye

Karin Boye: A Biographical Profile

1. *1900-1922*

Karin Boye was born on 26 October 1900, in the Swedish city of Göteborg. On her father's side she had German blood. Her paternal grandfather, Carl Joachim Eduard Boye, was the Prussian consul in the town. The Boye family originally came from Bohemia, and most of its male members devoted themselves to various forms of financial or commercial activity, both in Europe and in South America. As a young man, Eduard Boye was head of a large English clothes manufacturing business in Hamburg until the Great Fire of Hamburg in 1842 destroyed the office, warehouse and shops. He then moved to Leeds, in England, and took up clothes manufacturing there; later, he moved to Göteborg, where he was his firm's agent for a number of years. Eventually he established his own cotton and textile importing business in Göteborg, E. Boye & Co., and adopted Swedish citizenship in 1849. In addition to cotton importing, he also took an interest in industrial and marine engineering.

Eduard Boye was one of the pillars of Göteborg society, and together with his wife, Hilda, ran both a town and a country home in patriarchal style, entertaining many guests at dinners and soirées, and patronising the arts. They had five children, and it was their eldest son, Fritz (Carl Fredrik) who was Karin Boye's father. Fritz Boye trained at the Göteborg Technical High School as a civil engineer, practised as a draughtsman and designer at various works and plants, but eventually moved into the insurance business, becoming head of the Svea Fire-Life Company. He married Signe Liljestrand, an employee at his office, some eighteen years his junior – she made up in vitality and energy for his somewhat dour and retiring nature. The couple had several children, of whom Karin was the first. At first, her education was undertaken by her mother, who was very well-read in European classical literature and was also influenced by spiritualism and oriental religions. Her father remained a somewhat distant figure – his sons said later in life that they had never known him, and he seldom showed any tenderness towards his children. On the other hand, he possessed a speculative, imaginative mind, and even wrote a 'Fragment of a

---

* This account of Karin Boye's life is based on the information contained in Margit Abenius's Swedish-language biography *Drabbad av renhet* ('Afflicted by Purity'), published by Bonniers, Stockholm, in 1950.

Story About the Future', which is inspired by notions of utopian reform. His emotional instability and nervous temperament were perhaps the real reason why he found it difficult to come close to his children.

Karin Boye attended a private junior school in Göteborg. According to Karin Boye's biographer, Margit Abenius, her first teacher, Fröken Mimmie Agardh, had almost never had a pupil who stayed in her memory as Karin Boye did:

> The round, soft little girl was far ahead of her school-mates, she was remarkably well-informed and could answer any question, often did so with a little rhyme or other inventive and well-chosen words. Fröken Agardh offered to let her sit and read an interesting book while the others did their spelling, but Karin wanted to take part and help. Fröken Agardh especially remembers her delight at the spring. She would jump and rejoice: 'Aunt Mimmie, Aunt Mimmie, it's spring! How happy I am!' Jeanna Osterdahl also taught at the school, and Karin told 'Aunt' Jeanna that she wrote stories. Among her papers Fröken Agardh has preserved some short verses and fables by her pupil, including this 'Story of the Crocus, by Karin Boye, aged 7': 'There was once a little boy who had a little crocus. Inside the crocus there was a little elf; she could do magic spells. The crocus was yellow, and pretty. Now autumn came, and the crocus began to wilt. Krokusa (that was the elf's name) thought that was nasty, and flew away. Then the crocus fell. Have you seen a crocus fall?' The story is illustrated with a drawing of the flying Krokusa with a crown on her head, and underneath are the words: 'Krokusa flew away'.

In 1909 the family moved to Stockholm after Fritz Boye went into premature retirement because of nervous debility. This involved some reduction in the family's standard of living, but it did not affect the children's lives. Later on, Fritz Boye became an inspector in the Swedish Private Insurance Supervisory Service. At her new school, Karin made friends with a few girls of similarly introspective and imaginative temperament. Together they read the works of Dumas, Rudyard Kipling, H.G. Wells and Maeterlinck, and also those of Rabindranath Tagore. Tagore's poetry seems to have made an especially strong impression on the young Karin Boye: she immersed herself in Indian mythology, and sought to experience the country itself through Karl Gjellerup's Indian novel *Pilgrimen Kamanita* ('Kamanita the Pilgrim'). Above all, she studied Buddhism, and made serious efforts to learn Sanskrit. With her friend Signe Myrbäck as 'disciple', Karin played the role of guru, and the two girls would sit crosslegged on the lawn together, practising the art of breathing in and out. Signe Myrbäck relates that when their ecclesiastical history teacher once told the class that Sweden had only a small minority of Buddhists, Karin claimed to be one of them. Her history teacher, Lydia Wahlström, also once made some slightly disparaging remarks about Buddhists during a lesson, and Karin Boye put up her hand and said sternly: 'I'm a Buddhist!'

During her last two years at school, Karin Boye moved away from Buddhism and towards Christianity. Many of her schoolfriends found it hard to understand how she could have accepted Christianity, as previously she had always talked about it with cynicism and a kind of dry laughter. At first, the change seems to have been a source of happiness and self-discovery for her. Buddhism had become a life-denying influence on her, and for the first time she began to experience a sense of personal and inner freedom. At this time, she kept diaries. These are mostly of an "inner" nature, containing meditations on religious experience. In one passage she describes how she came to her religious awakening:

> Now I have reached the age of twelve or thirteen, the borderland between child and young person. Like a milestone shines the memory of one single book: Kipling's *Kim*. It is the last of my childhood books that I remember, and at the same time the one that probably meant most for my development.
>
> In the moving figure of Teshu Lama, religion entered my life for the first time as a living reality. That may seem strange for a child who had had a good Christian upbringing. But the child's religion is often so far from deserving the name 'religion' that it seems to me fruitless – with perhaps only a few exceptions – to offer a child the divine beauty of the Gospels, and a sacrilege to set the Gospel stories as homework. For me 'the Bible stories' were worn, everyday, already too well-known, when the hunger for religion began to awake. Teshu Lama – prepared by Puran Bhagat of *The Jungle Book* – came like a message from a world that had hitherto been closed, and I trembled, and I fell down and adored.

At the age of eighteen, she experienced a liberation and a transformation: an entry from the summer of 1918 reads: 'Domine, rex, venisti, vidisti, vicisti.' And on the eve of 1919: 'My birth-year is at an end.'

The diaries also concern Karin Boye's experiences not only at school, but also at Christian summer camps, where she seems to have approached the fairly routine group discussions with extraordinary intensity, forming close attachments to other girls and women in the groups. Two such relationships seem to have been particularly important for her. Agnes Fellenius, one of her classmates with whom she mutually shared all secrets, became quite severely depressed because of conflicts within her home, and Karin Boye took it upon herself to rescue her from the effects of this. She began to supervise Agnes' schoolwork, and made her take the final school examinations, trying by strength of willpower to make her pass, which she did. Margit Abenius describes how Karin stood outside the examination room, 'wrapped in intense concentration and the desire for a good outcome'.

The other important relationship was with Anita Nathorst, a woman who was seven years older than her and was a student of theology and the humanities at Uppsala University. At the Christian summer camp Karin attended at Fogelstad, Anita Nathorst was a group 'mother', looking after the young female students. Karin Boye wrote to her friend Signe Karlsson:

> Our 'mother' was Astrid Nathorst's sister, Anita Nathorst. Do you know who she is? Oh Signe, such a person! She is so wonderful! One day Ruth, Brita, Daisy and I carried blankets out into the park (it was immensely large) and took Anita with us and lay and talked. I don't think I shall ever forget it. I think I could dare to say all that I think and wonder to Anita and be certain that she would never misunderstand me. And one understands so well what she says. My goodness, it is not everyone of whom one can say that one understands what they mean.

By 1920, Karin Boye was a student at Uppsala University, and was herself a group mother at one of the meetings, held at Almnäs on Lake Vättern. It was at this meeting, with its 'question box', into which the schoolchildren put their questions about life and God, that Anita Nathorst helped her through her revulsion at, and fear of, human suffering, emotions that had led her to adopt Buddhism. A long letter from Karin Boye to Agnes Fellenius tells us something about the relationship between Karin and Anita:

> Then there was a question about the innocent suffering and death of creation. What it said, more or less, was: the animals eat one another. Can one hope for a continuation for the poor innocent victims? Can one believe that suffering has a meaning? Anita had the question and answered yes. She demonstrated that the lower life was sacrificed so that the higher could stretch ever further upward towards the divine, and she ended by reading a poem by Jeanna Oterdahl about a little boy who sits weeding in a garden plot, but suddenly feels sorry for the weeds. Then his mother says that the weeds will later become soil, and from the soil the beautiful flowers and the nice vegetables will get their nourishment. Must not the weeds like giving them their nourishment? Then the boy is pleased that he can help the weeds to become soil.
>
>   That answer acquired a deep significance for me. When I did not yet believe in God, I saw creation's innocent suffering and was horrified: that was why I so eagerly clutched at Buddhism's life-denying pessimism. Later, when I directly perceived life's value, I no longer dared to think of anything but human life. The other seemed terrible to me. Now I see suffering again – but in a different light.

> I said to Anita: 'Then that means that every meal we eat is a sacrament.' 'Of course,' she replied, 'have you never thought about it? That is why we say grace at table.' 'I have never understood why one ought to pray more there than elsewhere.' 'Formerly it was conceived as a sacrament. The first ritual action of the savage was shared meals. That is also the meaning of holy communion. The whole of life is a sacrament.'
>
> Do you understand this? Do you also understand how deeply this must move me? I fancied I saw the world in a new light – in the sign of the Cross, of representative suffering. God's cross extends through every time and every space. And what else is holy communion but an initiation to the Cross, the new union with God: one initiates oneself in order for His sake to take a part of His eternal suffering – upon oneself, to fight God's fight in the world: it involves great pain. I understood, or thought I understood, how Christ at the moment of communion gave himself as a sacrifice (oh, those old, worn-out phrases, something new shimmers through them now), when he said: 'This is my body – this is my blood.' Do you understand me? (NB You understand, I don't have in mind representative suffering as Anselm did, it is only this I mean: one person's suffering can serve and light the way for others.)

Karin Boye felt that her life was in some way mysteriously linked to the act of self-sacrifice, whether in the work of teaching to which she aspired, in her personal relationships, or in her writing. As a young student she underwent a severe inner crisis that was sparked by her decision to study, not theology, as the rector of her training college wished and advised, but psychology and teaching. This decision, which involved a dispute with and rebellion against the rector, also went against inner promptings which told her that to study theology would be true self-sacrifice, whereas psychology and teaching represented self-assertion. In a letter to Agnes Fellenius, Karin Boye says:

> For several days afterwards I wept like a rainy day in Göteborg. I prayed on my knees for guidance, but I received no direct revelation. A voice said: 'Sacrifice yourself! You, what are you? An ant. What are your possibilities? They must serve where they are needed, not where they would most fully develop. You must bow down, give up your will! Do you not see, it is in God's service? Your place is where you do good, not where you feel happy. Selfish, selfish creature!' But, much more loudly, self-assertion cried: 'I don't want to!'

One fundamental element of this crisis seems to have been Karin Boye's discovery of her own sensual and, more particularly, sexual self, and of the fact that her sexuality was oriented towards women, not men. If she chose the path of theology and a career in the church, she would have to deny that part of herself. To her, and to the artist in her, that seemed tantamount to denying *everything*. The startlingly direct and revealing letter to Agnes Fellenius continues:

Once before I cast a glance into myself, without on that occasion seeing in any way that within my religious and moral notions, within everything I had made mine *from without, without it being mine*, there was a reality that *conflicted* with this outward self, beautiful but not my own. You see, there has been a hard battle within me, and I have stood hesitating between whether to give up my will or to worship my will. Forgive me if I hurt you by writing this. You will quite certainly say that I did the wrong thing – I have chosen the latter.

One should perhaps say that there are two gods: the God whom we have created from our notions, and the God whom we do not know, but who creates us and is in us and wills in our wills and in all the world's will. Is that pantheism? Possibly. The most weighty consequence of the choice between them is this: in the first case there is a given morality, a fixed law (for me, who have received my image of God principally through the dreaming saints and the mystics: St Francis, Meister Eckhart, Mme Guyon, even Tagore, their experiences would therefore principally be laws). In the second case one has to follow oneself and be one's own law. Yes, of course – through one's conscience, you say. No. One's conscience may be split, divided between different psychic complexes. During this crisis I have had the conscience of a saint, which invited me to completely crush my will, take it as a sacrifice to God (which God? The created one! How otherwise would it be possible?) and a Nietzschean conscience, which invited me to take soundings of myself and make my innermost I into the highest law.

In this letter, which contains quotations from Nietzsche and Angelus Silesius, we find an early version of the poem 'Inwards', with its affirmation of '*my* truth/and *my* God'.

It was this crisis, in February 1921, that led Karin Boye to write the poems that are gathered in her first collection, *Moln* ('Clouds'). For her, it was as though a shell that had contained her had been cracked, and she began to realise her true subjectivity in symbols, images and forms. Her approach to God was that of the mystic, who proceeds not along the way of the grand and the transcendental, but in terms of the personal, the intimate and small. The discovery that she could by means of poetry rise above the dilemma that had tormented her, that she could sacrifice and serve as well as realise her gifts in art, must have been a profoundly life-altering experience for her. Yet still she doubted. When she took the manuscript of the poems to the distinguished Stockholm publisher K.O. Bonnier, she did not dare to go alone, but took her mother with her. Bonnier promised to read the poems, but warned her that 'so many people are writing poems just now, and no one buys poetry.' None the less, on 10 February 1922 she received a letter from Bonnier in which he confirmed that he had read the poems with great interest, and told her that she really could write poetry; he would publish the collection, though could not offer her more than 200 kronor by way of an advance. The reviews, when they came, were by and large good, though one, by a male reviewer, was snidely patronising, with an assertion that 'one should not expect too much when one opens a volume of poems with a woman's name on the title page'.

2. *1923-1932*

As a student of humanities at Uppsala University, her plans to become a teacher abandoned, Karin Boye began with the study of Greek, as she 'wanted to read Plato in the original'. In the Uppsala of the 1920s, with its receptivity to European influences and the readiness of a new generation to experiment with unfamiliar lifestyles and ideas, the passionate 'Teo', as Karin Boye soon came to be known by her fellow female students, was the subject of much interest and distant adulation. She made a striking visual impression on many who encountered her: there was something boyish about her, something inward-turned in a pre-Raphaelite manner, and it was an effect obviously achieved with conscious purpose. Though she could not be said to be beautiful in a conventional way, her face had an openness and a sensual prettiness that were given added fascination by the sense of intellectual clarity and emotional depth that lay behind them. She herself had certain reservations about her appearance, and beneath them lurked feelings of inferiority. These, Margit Abenius writes, 'concerned not her face but her figure, which she would have liked to be more supple and masculine. "It's a pity I'm so ugly," she told her friend Agnes. When Agnes Fellenius got engaged and the two were about to go their separate ways, she took a farewell photograph of Karin standing in bright sunlight against a white wall. Karin placed a hearth cushion over her feet because they were "so ugly", adding: "I want everything to be beautiful!"'

The second subject studied by Karin Boye was Nordic languages. In particular, she undertook the study of Icelandic, and thoroughly relished the prose and poetry written in it. The songs of the Edda made a lasting impression on her, and she wrote that the lectures about them were 'the only ones that go too quickly...the translation of a description of a chieftain: "Helgi rose high above chieftains as the nobly-born ash tree above the thorn bush or as a young deer, *dew-sprinkled*, rises above all other deer, and his horns burn high to heaven itself." It sounds better in Icelandic. And then, in the midst of it all, come barbaric, brutal similes, especially from the battlefields and their atrocities, but it is so magnificent, in spite of its nastiness, that one shivers with devotion...'

As her third subject, Karin Boye studied the history of literature, which she came to with great expectations but began to dislike because of the over-systematised nature of the teaching and its discouragement of independent thinking. She failed the first term examination in this subject, an experience that shocked her, who had never failed an examination before. In fact, her time at Uppsala University seems to have been spent less in formal study than in activity of an extra-curricular nature. In particular, she was secretary and later president of the students' union, where she also helped to organise discussion groups and theatrical events. At this time, too, she had a brief love affair with the poet Nils Svanberg. She was an eager participant in the activities of the students' 'messes' (*matlag*), which performed the function of societies, and were an important feature of Uppsala student life at this time. Karin Boye and Anita Nathorst belonged to the same society, and both were by now adherents of Freudianism. Many of the discussions held in the society concerned psychoanalysis, and although there is no evidence that Karin Boye was psychoanalysed at this time (though she was later), it would not have been surprising if she had made some experimental moves in this direction. She was also interested in the ideas of Adler.

During her last year at university, Karin Boye joined the idealistic peace organisation Clarté, which counted Ellen Key and Selma Lagerlöf among its members, and had a decidedly left-wing and anti-religious orientation. Many of those who knew her, including Anita Nathorst, were surprised at this step. It seems to have been motivated in part by Karin Boye's desire to assert herself as a 'normal' young woman, in tune with the progressive movements of her time. This desire for 'normality' almost certainly received impetus from her growing awareness of her inverted sexuality, which imparted an ever darker and more tragic note to the poems she was writing. She lived an emotionally strained existence, was prone to attacks of weeping, and came to rely more and more on Anita Nathorst for support and sympathy. Margit Abenius writes that 'Anita was able, in her austere way, to tell Karin a few home truths when her urge for unhappiness made itself felt. It could take strange forms of expression, as though she were positively looking for burdens to take upon herself. Was it the basically harmonious need of the one weighed down by guilt to "create happiness out of what one has broken" or merely the flagellant's desire for the lash, or was it the wish of a heroic soul armed with great strength to bear heavy woes, the certainty that in the hard and difficult one comes close to life's heart? Perhaps it was some of all this at the same time. Anita Nathorst brooded a great deal about how life was going to work out for Karin. It seemed as though she considered a marriage founded on friendship with a fatherly oriented man as the most practicable path. "But he will have to be understanding," these worried conversations concluded. "Good Lord, how understanding he will have to be!"'

The collection *Gömda land* ('Hidden Lands') was considered both by the critics and by the poet herself as somewhat 'better' than *Moln*, and indeed many of the lyrics make a stronger, less hesitant impression, though their tone is predominantly sombre. The influence of Freud may be seen in the concept of the 'hidden lands' which the poet makes it her task to discover – the journey is one towards the interior of the psyche. A key poem is 'Spring Song', with its assertion of a 'natural' freedom:

> In springtime, in sprouting time,
> the seed its shell destroys,
> and rye becomes rye and pine becomes pine
> in freedom without choice.

The poem is related to two diary entries about inner freedom, one from 1919, the other from 1920: 'Precisely in *the freedom of the will* (to choose) does our *unfreedom* lie. Freedom is to act in full accordance with one's nature: thus, true freedom has no choice, only one way to go.' 'Every action is unconditionally caused by inner or outer circumstances. But for that reason to call every action unfree is shortsighted. The will that is the deepest foundation of our being is naturally a natural product and none the less *our own ego*. Outside of this we possess no being. An action is *unfree* that is enforced not by our being's own nature but in conflict with it. But an action that is caused by *myself*, my will, is free.'

Another striking feature of the collection is the influence on it of Old Icelandic literature, in particular the poetry of the Edda. The qualities that seem to have attracted Karin Boye in these poems are the ones associated with emotional and spiritual directness, or 'erectness' or 'straightness' – *rakhet*. In 'Æsir and Elves' Odin hangs in the world tree 'erect' or – an image of unyielding hardness and inflexibility that may easily become fanaticism. This kind of emotional colouring becomes more and more frequent in Karin Boye's poetry as it develops, and it is possible to detect a connection between it and the poet's concern with issues of freedom, unfreedom and determinism. Her interest in left-wing, Marxist political theory and in Freudian psychology is rendered more comprehensible in this light. The dominant conflict in her work increasingly becomes that of a passionate, almost desperate desire for personal freedom and self-assertion with an awareness that such freedom may be impossible, and that the only solution is to submit to powers that are mightier than the human 'I'. It is a conflict that has its roots in the poet's personal crisis of 1921.

The poems of *Härdarna* ('The Hearths'), which was published in 1927, represent further evidence of the flow of poetic inspiration that visited Karin Boye during her years in Uppsala. The Swedish title has associations that are perhaps not so immediately evident in English – in Swedish, *härd* or 'hearth' can mean a seat, focus or centre, and the ancient 'hearths' the poet is trying to invoke are symbols of culture and the creation of culture throughout the ages. Perhaps the collection's most famous and characteristic poem is 'On the Move' (*I rörelse*), with its call for perpetual movement and quest:

> Yes, there is goal and meaning in our path –
> but it's the way that is the labour's worth.
>
> The best goal is a night-long rest,
> fire lit, and bread broken in haste.

One critic who noticed the originality of the new collection was Hagar Olsson, the friend and confidante of the Finland-Swedish poet Edith Södergran. In the newspaper *Svenska pressen* she wrote, under the headline 'New Tone in Swedish Poetry':

> One has long looked in vain for a sign of renewal within Swedish poetry. All the lights seemed to have gone out. The 'young generation' has displayed an aspect of effeteness, carefully concealed beneath a shimmer of echoes. One cannot characterise its striving better than with the catchword employed by Diktonius, 'rather pretty everyday product' [*vackrare vardagsvara*]. When one has with effort and a good deal of melancholy read Österling's new collection of poetry with the elegant title *Honour of the Earth* and the equally elegant publicity, one has said to oneself: will one single spark ever be lit in this suffocating atmosphere? Will there ever be a single lyre in the land of Sweden that is able to create life and tone in this oppressive, twilight-of-the-gods silence?
>
> Recently a small, unassuming collection of poetry appeared: *The Hearths*, by Karin Boye. No advertising surrounds it and the publicity states that the author is not one of the most prominent. But the cover shines with a brilliance that is different from and more enduring than that of fame: the brilliance of fire fighting its way through. One reads: Karin Boye, and it is with love that one commits it to memory. One thinks: here is one of the first swallows...

Swallow – that is perhaps the word for Karin Boye's poetry. It is not strong like the eagle; its wingbeat does not have that breadth and boldness – but neither does it belong to the grey and twittering breed of sparrows. It flies high and beautifully and the wind murmurs in its trembling wings...

These are different tones from those one is accustomed to hearing in modern standard-Swedish poetry. It is something that ignites, awakens, carries away, it is truly – poetry! One encounters here no aestheticised hypocrisy about a simple little everyday, a simple little home and a simple little happiness, one encounters an honest soul that looks with completely illusionless eyes on that which is, sees the inevitability of suffering and the vanity of happiness, but does not seek a port of refuge from it, rather instead prepares itself for – higher flight. One encounters for once a courageous spirit, one that has passed through the destruction of the 'I' without stopping at this, without complaining and feeling sorry for itself, finding its strength in a higher reality...

There is an extraordinary purity in this spirit, it is without fear and far from sentimentality. It is always ready for departure, that is its distinguishing mark... It is never tepid, never in two minds. It is in other words – inspired.

The poems singled out by Hagar Olsson for special praise in her review include 'On the Move', 'We Sleepy Children' and 'The Sea', which she called 'a proof of the lapidary strength of Karin Boye's style'. Though the reviewer considered the book uneven, the review article itself was probably responsible for confirming the poet on her path, and for establishing her as a major name among contemporary Swedish poets.

The years that followed were hectic ones, full of drama, both inner and outer. In 1927 Karin Boye's father, Fritz Boye, died of cancer. Immediately after graduating from Uppsala in 1928, Karin Boye moved to Stockholm, where she began a course of psychoanalysis with the analyst Alfhild Tamm, initially without her mother's knowledge. She took this first analysis very seriously, and could become quite upset if any of her friends criticised psychoanalysis, saying they could only do so if they tried it themselves. The work affected her quite deeply, and some of those who knew her considered that it changed her in many ways. Without it she would probably not have found her way to marriage, nor to the radical ideas that for a time were important to her.

In Stockholm, Karin Boye also became seriously involved with the organisation and administration of the Clarté movement, with which she had already come into contact in Uppsala. She also helped to edit the movement's magazine of the same title. The meetings and activities of Clarté, a loosely-organised assembly of some five or six hundred radical intellectuals and political activists from all over Scandinavia, were above all meant to free the minds of its members from the constraints of bourgeois upbringing, education and prejudice. There were two main strands of concern, both of which derived from the movement's central aim of establishing world peace and the happiness of human beings: one focused on the social transformation of the world, and the other was mainly preoccupied with questions of inner transformation by means of psychoanalysis. Among the Swedish members were the poets Gunnar Ekelöf, Nils Ferlin, Harry Martinson, and Karin Boye herself; among lesser-known names were the young poets Stellan Arvidson, Leif Björk, Ingeborg Björklund, Ebbe Linde, Arnold Ljungdal, Erik Mesterton, Ellen Michelsen, Victor Svanberg and Herbert Tingsten. Leif Björk, a young left-wing radical with an interest in psychoanalysis, became Karin Boye's partner, and after some time the couple married. Together with Björk and some other male Clarté members, Karin Boye visited the Soviet Union. It is probable that her experiences there stayed in her subconscious and influenced her in the writing, much later, of her novel about a totalitarian state, *Kallocain*.

Karin Boye's marriage to Leif Björk did not last long. The couple were too estranged from everyday reality, too over-complicated, and their household economy too precarious for this essentially bourgeois 'social form of love', as Margit Abenius calls it. In addition, it seems to have been more a friendship, or comradeship, than a marriage, and its sexual component was probably not very strong. Karin Boye had already experimented with one extra-marital affair, which brought her a disturbing sense of being hunted by the man for her innermost being. In order to escape having to surrender her inner self, she gave herself to him sexually, in body rather than spirit. These confusions and disturbances grew more frequent after the divorce from Leif Björk, and there were many more opportunities for casual relationships. In 1931 she fell into a severe depression, with suicidal phases. From a friend she obtained the name and address of a psychoanalytic doctor in Berlin.

Her analyst in Berlin, where she moved in January 1932, was Walter Schindler, a Freudian who used techniques of active suggestion. He considered Karin Boye's situation extremely serious, and found her a difficult patient. She herself suffered greatly during the two months of analysis, which came to an end after a crisis. After this, Karin Boye began to be analysed by a woman, Grete Lampl. Of the analysis with Schindler, Scharp noted in his diary that the analyst had said: 'This will end badly. Within ten years she will have taken her own life.'

Apart from analysis, Karin Boye's life in Berlin also involved work. She was an editor of the Swedish avant-garde literary magazine *Spektrum*, which modelled itself on Eliot's *Criterion*, and took its name from the idea expressed in one of her poems ('Man's Multiplicity'):

> In us a multiplicity lives.
> It fumbles towards unity.
> Its capturing, gathering burning-glass
> we were born to be

Spektrum published the early work of Gunnar Ekelöf, Harry Martinson, Karin Boye and other Swedish modernists; Karin Boye wrote editorials and essays and commissioned work on contemporary European poetry: Erik Mesterton's 'Poetry and Reality in Modern English Lyric Poetry' and 'The Method of T.S. Eliot' first appeared in *Spektrum*.

Karin Boye also worked as a literary translator, producing a Swedish version of Frieda Uhl's book about Strindberg. Little of this work brought in any money, however, and what with the expense of the psychoanalysis, the poet's financial situation was very precarious. She did, however, manage to see something of Berlin's theatre and café life, moved among male and female homosexuals, witnessed the clashes between extreme left-wing and right-wing sympathisers, and through Vilhelm Scharp, who knew the Swedish-born Göring, and also Goebbels, gained some insight into the true nature of Nazism. She even attended an election meeting in the Sportpalast at which the Shakespeare-admiring Göring used all his rhetorical skills to outmanoeuvre Hindenburg to Hitler's advantage. It is at this meeting that Karin Boye is reported to have raised her arm in the Hitler salute – not to do so could have cost her her life. Yet there is also some evidence to suggest that she found the mass spectacle fascinating, and that she found some release in surrendering herself to the well-directed and orchestrated cries of 'Die Treue ist der Mark der Ehre'. There is, however, no evidence of her ever having embraced the ideas of Nazism. Scharp related that they agreed during a conversation that 'it was impossible to unite a faith in man, his worth and personality, with obedience to dictatorship' (Margit Abenius).

In Berlin, Karin Boye also began a sexual relationship with Margot Hanel, a German-Jewish woman who was twelve years younger than her. It was a relationship that was to have a tragic end. In many ways, Karin Boye's life in Berlin was influenced by the confused and gloom-laden atmosphere of the last years of the Weimar

Republic, and her involvement with Margot Hanel was a part of that reality. The 'psychoanalytic' circles she frequented could not have been further removed from the Christian summer camps of her early twenties; while the contrast was necessary and salutary, there are also some factors that suggest her life might have taken a more fortunate turn had she avoided those circles.

3. *1933-1938*

One of the ways in which Karin Boye sought to clarify the problems in her inner and emotional life, and even to seek answers to them, was the writing of prose fiction. In novels such as *Crisis*, *Astarte* and *Merit Awakes*, she explored the themes of the strong woman and the weak man, of lifelong self-deception, of the 'doll's house', and other problems of inner and outer existence. These works, of which she wrote many, are less "pure" than her poetry. They are often somewhat schematic, and the characters tend to be merely vehicles for the author's ideas. From many angles these works can even be viewed as commercial, which they were insofar as another aim of her writing them was to secure herself an income, a task made all the more pressing by the expense of analysis. Yet in these books she tackled themes that were controversial in their time, and she probably helped others by publishing them. This was particularly true of *Crisis*, a book which depicts her own adolescent religious crisis and discovery of her own bisexuality. Around 1933, at the time it was written, there was much discussion in Sweden about a liberalisation of the laws on homosexuality, and her documentary novel was a contribution to the public debate. It is probably her strongest prose work after her masterpiece, *Kallocain*, and it was widely read and discussed.

Back in Sweden in 1934, the poet bought a small flat in Stockholm consisting of two rooms and a kitchen ' in an environment so devoid of tradition, more functionalistically cold and impossible than anywhere else in Stockholm...a hell of lines that gives not the slightest opportunity to the imagination'. According to Margit Abenius, however, the flat possessed a good view in summer of flowering gardens and a fountain, and it is possible that Karin Boye felt less lonely in a city than she might have done living alone in the countryside. There was, nevertheless, the fact that all her attempts to make a life with another human being had failed. Temperamentally unsuited to solitariness, she must have found her life at this time extremely difficult. In desperation, she decided to invite Margot Hanel to come from Berlin and live with her. At first the experiment went well: for the first time in her life, Karin Boye felt calm and reassured, and as if she had some sort of root in existence. But Margot Hanel was extremely jealous and dependent, and as time went by she began to develop chronic illnesses, making Karin look after her and take complete responsibility for her. In a matter of months, the 'marriage' degenerated into a destructive symbiosis: while, out of jealousy, Margot refused to let Karin see her literary friends and tried to make her stay in the flat and talk about trivia, Karin repaid her with personal cruelty, talking to others condescendingly about her, and even calling their relationship 'ein ausgehaltenes Verhältnis'. Yet the couple stayed together. Karin evidently found in Margot, who made such very great demands on her, an outlet for her need for self-sacrifice and self-immolation. Margot Hanel also seems to have been a substitute for the child Karin Boye never had. And, while it must have been profoundly tormenting for both partners much of the time, the relationship also had its brighter moments. According to Margit Abenius, the couple 'became welded together in the way that cannot be avoided between two people who share life's troubles for a long time'. It was to Margot Hanel that Karin wrote the epigram 'To You':

> You my despair and my strength,
> you took all the life I owned,
> and because you demanded everything,
> you gave back a thousandfold.

At this time, also, Karin Boye wrote her novel *Too Little*. Its hero, Harald Måhrman, is torn between art and life, and ends by choosing neither, creating an atmosphere of disharmony and hostility wherever he goes. His failure is a failure to love – either his art or his family, or both. Margit Abenius quotes Karin Boye's diary of 1921, with its entry: 'I believe that what one receives in love is precisely what one gives – not necessarily from and to the other person, but from and to love.'

1935 saw the publication of Karin Boye's fourth book of poetry, *För trädets skull* ('For the Tree's Sake'). This met with a mixed response from the critics, many of whom saw in it a capitulation to free-verse modernism. In fact, however, the volume continues and develops many of the poet's earlier themes and concerns, though now with more austere technical means, and an almost "neo-classical" restraint. The free verse poems give the impression of avoiding rhyme and metre in order to approach the truth more closely, not in order to shock, or to disrupt conventional modes of perception. One detects a shift away from Christianity, and at the same time away from the ideals of Clarté towards a more abstract, impersonal kind of art – yet the familiar themes of love, suffering, sacrifice, hope and betrayal are always present, too. Much of the negative thrust of the critics' response to the collection – they wanted the "old" Karin Boye back – was precisely because she had moved on from political radicalism towards an individually-conceived view of the world and of cosmic reality.

Margit Abenius describes a dream which Karin Boye related to Harry Martinson: 'She was dead and had come to paradise. Heavenly bliss was organised like a school. On the wall hung a timetable showing hours and lessons. Karin and the other blessed ones had to sit in the chalices of sweet-scented roses and God hurled the roses with their souls through the azure. A radiant, unutterable sense of happiness accompanied the rose lesson. After that came the 'lily lesson'. Brilliant white madonna lilies grew everywhere in large clumps and clusters as far as the eye could see. One could hear singing. Pilgrims walked in multitudes. But the lily lesson was not as eventful and highly-charged as the rose lesson; it led nowhere but seemed to stand still. Then an immensely large female figure appeared. She was wonderfully beautiful, but her hands were large and coarse like a charwoman's. Karin knew that this was Reality. She suddenly saw this hybrid of goddess and charwoman sitting on a throne, and seized by reverence she bowed down and kissed her foot. And then Reality asked: "Why are you kissing my foot? After all, you do not know me."'

In 1936, Karin Boye started work as a teacher at Viggbyholm boarding school, near Stockholm. The school's founder, a Christian pacifist named Per Sundberg, wanted to bring together children from different ethnic backgrounds, and many of the pupils were refugees from Hitler's Germany. There were also many children of divorce, and children with problems of development. At first, Karin Boye went on living in Stockholm and travelling to the school to teach, but eventually she moved to Viggbyholm and spent all her time there. It was a milieu that brought together several of the previous environments in which she had lived: the radical, pacifistic intellectual atmosphere was reminiscent of that of Clarté, while the Christian element in the teaching was similar to what she had experienced as a young theology student at summer camps. There was also the presence of trees and nature. Initially, Karin Boye taught very young children. There were problems attendant on this, however, for the children tended to laugh at their teacher and call her names. One little boy even said, when the children were asked why they laughed at her: 'because she looks like a little pig!' Thereafter, Karin Boye was transferred to the school's higher classes, the 'gymnasium', or grammar school, where she became a much-admired and loved teacher.

Far from being the 'school of reality', however, this was hardly an ordinary environment. In many ways, it seems to have functioned in Karin Boye's life as a kind of continuation of her psychoanalysis: spending so much time in the company of children and young people, she found that new layers of her personality were constantly being opened. This process of 'opening' or 'being broken open' had become very important to her: 'All human beings want to be broken open,' she wrote to her friend Anna Petri. At this time, too, she developed a lively interest in Gestalt psychology.

Among the German-Jewish emigré friends she made during the summer of 1937 time were several men. To one of these she became very closely attached, and it seemed that some kind of decision was imminent. But at the last moment the poet went away to Stockholm to see Margot Hanel for a few days, and when she came back she asked the man to forget everything that had passed between them. Something seemed to have changed in her relationship with Margot, and from that time onwards she ceased to talk of it and her in condescending tones. The epigram 'To You', written in July 1937, put the seal on this. Yet the problems within the relationship were not resolved: indeed, they seemed to intensify. In 1938 Karin tried to send Margot to Paris to live with a family there, but Margot returned within a month. Karin spoke of 'events that have made my life into chaos', and in a letter to the handwriting expert, Dr Blum she wrote, in German:

> Nur tun mir Ihre Schlussworte über die notwendige Resignation ein bisschen weh. Ich stehe eben in einer Situation, wo eine absolute Selbstaufopferung – von Arbeitsfreude, Kameradschaft, künstlerischem Schaffen, Ruhe, Harmonie – verlangt wird, und ich habe so schwer ein solches Opfer zu bringen, jedenfalls kann es nicht mit Freude geschehen. Glauben Sie wirklich, dass Resignation der Sinn meines Lebens sein kann? (Eine zu persönliche Frage... Die Antwort kann nie von einem Anderen kommen.)

> Only your words at the end about necessary resignation hurt me a little. For I am in just such a situation where an absolute self-sacrifice – of joy in my work, of friendship, of artistic creation, of peace, of harmony – is demanded of me, and I find it so hard to make such a sacrifice – at any rate, it cannot happen with joy. Do you really believe that resignation can be the meaning of my life? (A too personal question... The answer can never come from someone else.)

In February 1938, Karin Boye visited the cathedral town of Linköping in order to give a reading of her poems. While staying there, she visited the cathedral and had a deep spiritual experience while standing before the altar-painting of Christ by the modern Norwegian artist Anna Sørensen, and the tapestries by Märta Afzelius. The result of the experience forms the subject of the long poem 'Linköping Cathedral', in *The Seven Deadly Sins*.

During the summer of the same year, the poet visited Greece on a travel scholarship from the Swedish Academy. On the way she visited Vienna, Prague and Istanbul. In Greece she travelled from Athens to Delos, where she wrote: 'the Aegean sea is brilliant blue, and on the other side of the water lie other rocky islands in a thick heat haze. The light is wonderful. It overwhelms one, takes one's breath away. It is apt here. After all, Apollo was the one "whose eyes had never seen the darkness".'

In the autumn of 1938, at her own request, Karin Boye took up full-time teaching at Viggbyholm, but the workload proved to be too much for her, and she suffered from overstrain and exhaustion. Her consciousness of the cruel and terrible events that were taking place in Europe at this time, the German invasion of Czechoslovakia and the persecution of the Jews, also contributed to her sense of confusion and breakdown. She was unable to write or work on her poetry, a condition which for her was tantamount to a complete paralysis of spirit, and she developed a severe and acutely painful inflammation of the nerves in one of her arms, which nothing would cure. Eventually she left Viggbyholm, and returned to Stockholm.

4. *1939 – Summer 1941*

It was at around this time that the poet began to correspond again more frequently with Anita Nathorst, whom she had now known for almost twenty years. Anita had contracted a disastrous form of skin cancer, which was eating its way inwards into her body. Karin, who was still in love with Anita, travelled to Alingsås, near Göteborg, in order to be with her and look after her. While she was there, she wrote letters to Margot Hanel assuring the latter of her continued loyalty. In many ways, the poet seemed split in two – something noticed by her mother, who wanted to encourage her daughter's move away from Margot Hanel, but was concerned by her psychological state. This may not have been made any easier by the fact that Anita was by now the assistant of the psychoanalyst

Iwan Bratt, who lived in Alingsås and whose house she frequented. Karin came into contact with many seriously disturbed patients, and Bratt himself seems to have been a somewhat controversial figure, with an approach to psychoanalysis that some called crude and oversimplified.

Nonetheless, all this time Karin Boye continued to work at her writing with great application and an almost demonic intensity. Not only did she produce a large body of poetry – she also wrote and completed her prose masterpiece, the novel *Kallocain*, which bears a motto from T.S. Eliot:

> The awful daring of a moment's surrender,
> which an age of prudence could never retract,
> by this, and this only, we have existed...

Kallocain, a strange, nightmarish novel of cells and staircases and corridors, is open to several interpretations. On one level, it may be read as a political satire in the tradition of Zamyatin's *We* or Huxley's *Brave New World*: it concerns events within a World State of the future, which resembles both the Third Reich of the Nazis and the Soviet Union of Stalin. A central role is played by a truth serum ('Kallocain') invented by Leo Kall, a worker in a state chemical plant, who seeks to overthrow the state and the lies with which it has indoctrinated humanity. On another level, however, the novel may be read as a meditation on inwardness and confession, or 'breaking-open'. It contains many passages of extreme power and evocativeness, underscored by the eerie presence of wartime Sweden, with its military personnel on the streets, its whispered conversations held in fear of being overheard.

When it appeared in the autumn of 1940, *Kallocain* met with enthusiastic reviews. Artur Lundkvist declared that it was in 'the international class', while another critic called it 'a thoroughly thought-through, thoroughly felt, one might even say thoroughly suffered work of art'. The poet herself wrote to Ingeborg Holst on 23 January 1941:

> You asked me how it (the novel) had gone and how it had been received. It has had consistently excellent reviews and has even come out in a second edition...All kinds of people, friends and strangers alike, have written and thanked me...

As Margit Abenius writes in her biography, both *Kallocain* and the poems of *The Seven Deadly Sins* should be seen as the fruits of the liberation experienced by Karin Boye when she perceived that 'our most intimate and most extreme problems are and remain problems of life-philosophy and faith': 'It was an image of man that was formed in her view of life – an image that has probably always been there in rough outline – a Spinozan image, in which man is a multiplicity of countless forces that strive towards the 'unity' which it reflects in its broken life-utterances. In 'Man's Multiplicity' the prophetess speaks as out of a dark Middle Ages:

> We were born of mothers of heaven and earth
> and of powers with no end in view,
> nocturnal wills and wills of light
> with names that no one knew.
>
> May one of the many
> not gain power over us,
> though she be of heaven's race
> and shine in magnificence.
>
> In us a multiplicity lives.
> It fumbles towards unity.
> Its capturing, gathering burning-glass
> we were born to be.
>
> Great is man's striving,
> great the goals it has set –
> but much greater is man himself
> with roots in universal night.
>
> So give, that we shield a secret room
> and never a flame do lack
> on the altar of an unknown god,
> that may tomorrow wake.

The last year of Karin Boye's life was one of tragic contrasts, paradoxes and deepening insight. Realising the depth of her love for Anita Nathorst, she also realised that that love could not be returned to her. In a letter to a friend, she wrote:

> That not even the times and the decline of the West should prevent one from collapsing like a house of cards and burning like a piece of tinder and that when one finally attains something that has lain in one for twenty years, the person concerned is dying of cancer and sufficiently exposed to radium not to have a spark of sex left. We agreed that life is macabre in a way that no reforms can ever remove, macabre to its innermost kernel.

Yet this was also the year in which she visited Denmark, which was now under German occupation. Conscious of the propaganda value of cultural visits, the German authorities in Copenhagen had arranged for a delegation of German writers and poets to come and give readings there. No one attended them. Then the Danish cultural authorities invited a group of Swedish poets and writers, including Karin Boye, to take part in a 'Swedish week' in the Danish capital. Karin Boye was introduced to the Danish royal family, and *Kallocain* was written about enthusiastically in the Danish press. This visit was perhaps the nearest the poet ever came to a direct political action, and it also set the seal on her fame and international reputation. She is now considered one of the major Swedish poets of all time, in the same tradition as Viktor Rydberg, Gustaf Fröding and Vilhelm Ekelund. She was also a seminal influence on the development of Swedish modernism, in particular the generation of 1940s poets that included Gunnar Ekelöf, Harry Martinson, Erik Lindegren and Artur Lundkvist.

The inner conflicts that split Karin Boye and which were reflected in her tortured love relationships gained the upper hand over the artist in her. Inwardly doubting about Anita, whose move away from Alingsås to Malmö may not have been entirely for medical reasons, and deeply ambivalent about Margot Hanel, who was still completely emotionally dependent on her, Karin Boye succumbed to an access of despair. On 23 April 1941 she left the house at Alingsås and walked off into the surrounding countryside, taking only a bottle of sleeping tablets with her. Some days later, after a police search of the district that proved fruitless, she was found by a passer-by, dead from exposure. A month later, Margot Hanel gassed herself. Anita Nathorst died of cancer in August.

DAVID McDUFF

CLOUDS
(1922)

Clouds

See the mighty clouds, whose distant lofty tops
proud, shimmering rise, white as white snow!
Calmly they glide on, at last in calm to die below,
slowly dissolving in a shower of cool drops.

Majestic clouds – smiling onward they go straight
through life, through death in brilliant sun,
in ether so clear and pure, dark care unknown,
with quiet and grand contempt for their fate.

Would I were granted, festively proud as those,
to climb where the bustle of worlds does not tread
and bear the sunlight's golden wreath around my head
no matter how angrily round me the storm's roar goes.

A Buddhist Fantasy

Unlocked is the world's copper gate.
High in its gate-vault here I stand,
and what I see is infinitely great,
and no sight is so without end.

However deep I look, however far,
my gaze receives no help beneath.
All that I know exists no more –
not great, not small – not life, not death.

One single step on pathways free,
and for me all return is closed...
Why do you quake? Up, follow me!
For the universe's copper gate is forced!

The Nightjar

Half awake the summer night broods
quietly on dreams that no one knows.
The tarns' glistening floods
reflect a twilight sky's
infinity, pale, morose,
Whiter grow the stars on high.
Afar, afar
the nightjar
sings alone her toneless, comfortless melody.

Never boldly, towards the heights she swings,
because of her lowness hovers low.
Downy twilight wings
seem bound to the earth,
by dust and soil weighed down below.
Woe to him whose wings in pair
cannot rise,
only linger,
helplessly drawn to the mud, whose colours they bear.

But the whitest of white among swans,
that travel in morning's bright space
their royal lanes,
never cherished a yearning
such as the nightjar has.
None has a longing so true
for the distant and far
as the nightjar
for the ever beckoning, ever yielding blue.

To a Sphinx

You are like the mollusc in chilly ponds
where sunbeams never get.
She never creeps out from her shell,
her prison she cannot forget,
she can only hide
her deepest essence
and dream of exploits great
among the waterweed,
but never wholly
and undividedly
empty herself into word or deed.

With irony your speech full spills.
You try to cover
with pretended cold
life's warmth that inside dwells.
But your voice trembles,
is strangely weak,
A blush hovers
behind each pale cheek.
A sea of fire burns
in a secret place
that no one knows,
no one can trace.

You are too frail and too weak and tame
for all the discords that sever:
to wear armour you must endeavour
in life's hard-handed game.
You are like the mollusc in chilly ponds
that never creeps out of her shell,
so unattainable,
so incomprehensible,
that no one will near you, ever.

Idea

Here I go not. This is not I.
This is a lying reflection alone,
asking, wondering where I have gone,
yearning one day to meet its reality.

The legend tells: far in a distant land
flows a mirroring flood from invisible source.
Thousands of beings, blessed, holy souls,
lean like lilies o'er the banks of sand.

Light without limit envelops their eye,
air trembles, sated by a beauty without like.
In this realm perfect spirits walk,
There stands in eternal light my true I.

The reflection is gone from the glittering surge.
It was once torn away by the angry stream,
wanders around, unreal as in a dream,
unfinished, broken, of itself in search,

Do I not hear the flood's waves far away?
Deep from my inmost depths its water flows.
There, where life's swell into day breaks and goes,
it waits for me concealed, my god-begotten I.

Evening Prayer

No time is like this one,
the evening's final, silent hour.
No sorrows burn any longer,
no voices crowd any more.

Then take now into your hands
this day that is past, like a token.
For I know: into good you will turn
what I have held or broken.

Evilly I think, evilly I act,
but all things you heal and cleanse.
My days then you transform
From gravel to precious stones.

You must lift, you must carry,
I can only leave all things behind.
Take me, lead me, be close to me!
Show me what you next may intend!

Crossroads

Candles I saw burning, yes, holy candles on the eternal mountaintops.
Blessed ones walked there in a trembling mystic light,
radiant with God as with the sun the falling drops,
radiant with sleep in worlds where time was not.

Woe is me, my foot is too heavy for those giddying high paths,
woe is me, who was formed from clay and whose thought is steel and
    stone!
Never will I find a place among those dreaming holy silent ones,
never will my head by seeing's halo be crowned.

You will I seek, my God, in the simple, the grey, despised,
you will I seek in the world, in the everyday's striving and plight.
The sky's golden stillness, to which my heart aspired,
is it better than your labour, your holy, burning fight?

Lord, your bliss is yours. You gave, and you took, and you hide
    yourself.
Give what you offer – not peace, but your fight, and your spirit to
    fulfil.
Lord, on the world's battlefield like sword or bow I follow you.
Give me a throne, if you wish, or a cross, if you will!

The Best

The best that we possess,
we cannot give away.
we cannot write it either.
and neither can we say.

The best that is in your mind
no one can make unclean.
It shines there deep inside
for you and God alone.

It is the glory of our wealth
that no one else can gain it.
It is the torment of our poverty
that no one else can attain it.

Morning Song

This is life's silent hour,
sunny and blessed,
laughing white in power-conscious peace.
The rejoicing and the songs fell silent,
for Joy overflowed the shores.
Hail to you, Joy, Joy,
in your silent, vainglorious smile!
You alone can plumb
the secret of the worlds.

O bubbles, bubbles, o foam, foam
are all our care, all our grief,
yes foam on measureless expanses,
bubbles on the ocean
is that which we chase and cherish and fear,
but Joy, Joy is the world's foundation.

How do I dare...? And yet!
Do you think that life's flower,
carved a thousand times by suffering.
would continue in darkest darkness
to shine in beauty in spite of everything,
were not its root and heart
heavy, yes, brimful of bliss?

O bubbles, bubbles, o foam, foam
is all our pain, our blind grief.
Joy alone knows more than others.
Yes, in its holy white hours
rests in the leaves' quivering daylight
the reflection of godlike depths,
smiling, smiling.

Like tidal waves, like thunderclouds
day's care will soon envelop me.
Let me remember in tears and greyness,
that clarity's blinding moment
forced me to say to life and death,
to the whole world and even to myself:
'Amen, amen,
happen, then!'

Early Spring
(A Painting in Pre-Renaissance)

A veil-light mist stands over the meadow,
and pearl-grey dew sprinkles pale leaves –
a spring morning, cool and melancholy-glad,
when airy flowers unfold from humid groves.

In the grass narcissi dully gleam in rows.
From fragile chalices a scent of spring spreads down,
when over them with dreamy gaze there goes
a noble boy from Arno's town.

A happiness of wonder rests upon his face.
His walk is full of awkward charm and pliancy.
A book he bears, as careful as a sage.

He scarce perceives the meadow's paradise,
but stares foreboding-pale as the spring day
at mysterious distance, hidden in morning haze.

A Painter's Wish

I would like to paint a meagre fragment
of the shabbiest everyday, so worn and grey,
but radiant with that fire that made
the whole world leap from the Creator's hand.
I would like to show how what we disdain
is holy and deep and the Spirit's attire.
I would like to paint a wooden spoon in such a way
that people had an inkling of God!

To an Unknown Descendant

I broke my bread which others' hands had to bake,
and drank my wine, which I did not prepare.
Those who had the toil never got to taste
its fruit, before they trod on dark roads there.

What I have sown, tomorrow you will harvest.
Oh may my seed an hundredfold bear deep!
They bear delight, who bear others' burdens.
they harvest life, who others' harvests reap.

Inwards

My God
and *my* truth
I saw
in a strange hour.
People's words
and commands were silent.
Good and evil
my soul forgot.
My God
and *my* truth
I drank
in the hour of my anxiety.

My God
was salt darkness,
my truth
hard metal.
Deeply I shook.
Naked I stood,
washed by waves
of cold truth,
cold, strong,
contemptuous truth –
my Truth
and *my* God.

Bare Frost

Gold and pale copper! Hoar frost on fields of brown gold!
The wide and golden world is glittering cold.

Through the clouds I see rivers, of sun and gold they are made,
forcing through, laughing chill as their wills' sharpened blade.

Smiling, defiant, breaking forth through the spaces it goes,
sunbeam-yellow and frosty round meadows and fields it flows.

Hear, sound it acquires, and the clear expanses rejoice!
Hear how, to reply, the whole world receives a singing voice!

A thousand times beaten and sacked and put to the knife
defiant she sings the songs of eternal desire for life.

The Spring's Expectancy

Do I not walk here drunken with fragrance of roses
– yet no roses have come! –
Does not all tremble, wrapped in divine gossamer?
The reflected light whispers secret promises.

From far away a wind reached me lately,
light as a held-back breath,
full of a fragrance of shyly trembling expectancy.
Ever since then I have sensed a miracle.

I know nothing – walk as in a far-off land,
walk as in a dream, a dream of roses.
All is as before – yet all is changed.
Strange mystery over things!

Wish-Night

If a star comes loose
and falls white through the air,
then, it is said, she answers our prayers, that reach
that short glimmering path.

I wait and wait. It is April,
a warm and sharp-eared night in April,
when the grass grows and the stars listen –
tonight they go so peacefully their way,
and not one trips and falls!

But if I fall asleep, it matters not at all:
if a star tears itself loose tonight,
then she must feel my prayer, where she descends,
even though I sleep –
for all the silent, silent night
all of wide, wide space
is completely full of my only wish!

O a blade...

O a blade,
yieldingly supple and strong,
o a lithely dancing blade,
proudly obeying the sternest law,
the rhythm's hard law in the steel –
o a blade
I would be in body and soul!

You I hate,
you my wretched willow-being,
you that twine, you that twist,
patiently obeying others' hands.
You I hate,
you my lazy dreamer-being.
You shall die.
Help me, my hatred, you sister of longing,
help me to become
a blade, yes a blade,
a dancing sword of hardened steel!

You

Cool is your voice as murmur of springs, and your being
tartly fresh as the autumn's fragrant fruits.
Clear in your eye rests
high September's chill merriment.

A fountain you are, whose sunnily glittering beam,
beautiful in its equilibrium, beautiful in its form-strict arc,
beautiful in its strength, possesses
the power to love limits and noble dimensions.

Hail to your playing calm, your springtime health!
Hail to your spirit's sweet, godlike nobility,
drawn in your features' purity
and the singing harmony of your limbs!

Morning

When the morning's sun steals through the window-pane,
happy and cautious,
like a child who wants to surprise
early, early on a festive day –
then I stretch full of growing exultation
my open arms to the coming day –
for the day is you,
and the light is you,
the sun is you,
and the spring is you,
and all of beautiful, beautiful
waiting life is you!

Dream

Twilight over an unknown path...
Colourless earth-plants,
great mushrooms
sprout from the ground, where sound is choked.
Winding naked trunks
stretch up and vanish in the darkness.
Hear the fearful roar up there,
that never falls silent!

Just now in the sun
I sang on flowering meadows
Pan, Pan, the great Pan.
Scornfully whisper now
the marshes' murmuring bubbles:
'Here in the forest of the secret depths,
here too is his dwelling!
Do you still dare to sing
Pan, the great Pan?'

Help, my foot is sinking!
Quagmire is the ground.
Brooding lurk
black waters, half in sleep,
unmoving, unfathomable,
in wait for me, their prey.
The snakelike trunks of the alders,
grown out of the wet marsh,
twist wailing this way and that.
Fear stretches from muddy water
hands, black and gnarled,
like the damp-dripping
rotten branches on which the moss grows.
Help, oh, help, what secret
depths, that desire me!

Yet – is that not the scent of flowers?
All around above dark marshes
buds gleam,
white buds –
oh, they unfold, they shimmeringly unfold!

My foot finds a hold among white chalices,
and over the depths moves a light –
the sweetest mocking smile.

Bow down, heart,
bow down and pray!
Here in the forest of the secret depths
I sing Pan
I sing trembling
Pan, Pan, the great Pan!

To Beauty

When our gods fall
and we stand alone among wreckage,
as much without a hold for our feet any longer
as spheres in space –
then you are dimly seen for a moment, lofty Beauty.
Then, only then.
As stern as fire you speak consolation:
'Whatever else falls – I remain.'
O stay, stay, holy one,
and save my soul
from the falsehood of a measureless sorrow!

Memory

Quietly would I thank my fate:
never do I lose you entirely.
As a pearl grows in the mussel,
so within me
grows your dewy essence sweet.
If at last one day I forget you –
then you will be blood of my blood,
then you will be one with me –
may the gods grant that.

The Exhortation

'Child!' said Life to me one day.
'How young you are! A little unripe fruit...
I want to teach you the adornment of youth:
modest discretion,
lowered eyes and quiet voice.
Go softly now – go on tiptoe over the meadows!
Silent, be silent – hold your breath and listen!
If Joy greets you, if Pain greets you,
don't make such a dreadful fuss (you usually do)!
Be infinitely quiet! Listen! Listen!
Then perhaps you will
find the way home to my rose-garden.'

Recovery

You who are called by the names of flowers,
now I want to give you another:
The Surgeon's Knife.
A cold, hard name.
But so gleamingly hard
is your image in the silent hours.
I am doomed when I see you,
doomed like one who is sick
before your health of springtime morning.

It is good that one suffers and sickens.
You are refreshingly free from mercy
towards torments of pathos.
Afar, afar you smile mysteriously.
I would breathe your lofty air.
I would tread those dewy paths
where you walk.

The Doors

I love those white mountains, the marble white
with foreheads rinsed by the heavens' high blue repose,
and the storming glitter of the salt sea,
and Doric temples, and thought's cool crystal.

But I have also lingered by doors left ajar
and seen inside, into sounding twilight depths,
where the shimmer of altar candles quietly rejoiced
in the face of trembling time, Advent,
while the winter morning stared dark through vaulted windows.

Those radiant saints, those who overcame,
could be sensed, blessed, beyond the darkness,
and God's yearners
bent their knees in prayer, lonely in their hosts,
and saw with closed eyes the Only One's brilliance,
the soul's innermost worlds,
and mystical truths they learned listening.
If you have ever listened near burning altar candles,
then you will never forget God's silent, blossoming gardens –
you will kiss the stone of the gate-arch and turn away.
White mountains, marble white in dazzling sun,
beloved, distantly-seen, my home in presentiment,
I come to you!
Life is to cut and to break so that something may grow.
Everyone is so many people,
but more than one road no one goes.

Homeless

To lose the soul's home and to wander far
and then be unable to find anything else,
and feel that one's forgotten what truth is,
and fancy one is made of nought but lies,
be sickened by oneself and hate oneself –
yes, that is easy, that is very easy.
Sorrow is easy, but joy is proud and hard,
for joy, it is the simplest thing of all.

But he that seeks for himself a home
must not believe that it exists just anywhere –
he *must* go wandering homeless for a time;
and he that's made of lies and would be well,
must hate himself until the day he knows
of truth what others as a gift receive.
What point is there in grieving so for it?
Wait then, my heart, and have some patience yet!

If this life is the only one...

If this life is the only one...!
Oh, these short hours...
An hour – how much an hour can become!
Those deep springs where no one yet has drunk,
the light-expanses no one yet has fathomed,
And we, we dully doze in cowardice.
Oh, these short hours...
O world of hidden possibilities,
O God in the becoming,
give us an undaunted piety,
a pure will,
and initiate us to the adventure of the spirit!

Small Things

If you cannot manage one step more,
cannot lift your head,
if you are sinking wearily under hopeless greyness –
then be thankful for the kind, small things,
consoling, childish.
You have an apple in your pocket,
a book of stories there at home –
small, small things, despised
at the time, that radiated living
but gentle footholds during the dead hours.

Saved

The world streams with dirt, emptiness fills it.
Wounds that the day made heal when evening is at hand.
Calm, calm, I lean my head
on a holy vision, your lingering memory.
Temple; refuge; purification;
my sanctuary!
On your steps saved from the darkness
secure as a child I fall asleep.

Awakening

Life acquires a different hue –
trembling, trembling it listens and is silent,
when like the shimmer from Vättern's stone in the folktale
the thought of you from the depths
rises wholly through-annealing all the world.
Newly-awoken I see reality,
where aching dreams burdened me just now.
The air is living, life I breathe,
life from you, from you.

Explanation

In your beauty submerged
I see life explained
and the dark riddle's answer
made plain.

In your beauty submerged
I want to say a prayer.
The world is holy,
for you are there.

Endless with brightness,
light-engorged,
I would die with you,
in your beauty submerged.

You Are My Purest Consolation

You are my purest consolation,
you are my firmest protection,
you are the best thing I have,
for nothing hurts like you.

No, nothing hurts like you.
You smart like ice and fire,
you cut like a steel my soul –
you are the best thing I have.

The Maple

Hail to those warriors who bleed in the battles,
in spite of scars and wounds shining,
hail to their hard struggle,
hail to their dearly bought victories!

But O young tree, you blossoming maple,
you I love more than warriors' scars.
Your unacquired, happy nobility
is greater than their won battles.

Fresh in life's morning you sprouted from the earth,
fresh, fresh you grew calmly in sun and rain;
anguish you did not know, nor remorse,
nothing of all our sickness.

You blossom in gold and gold vine; in sighings you laugh,
when the wanderer kisses your trunk.
His kiss is a prayer to the eternal beauty
your lovely blossoms thought in the day.

Blessed be, blessed be, fair-growing maple!
You do not need the combatants' victories.
In you is the repose of lonely forests.
In you is sun of divinity.

Dream Vision

Dream vision, dream vision,
sun-clear revelation,
lit for my gaze by a single
human creation,

dream vision, dream vision,
sweet among fighters maimed,
sweet in a torn-apart
world of pain.

dream of a race
growing forth through the ages,
proud people, who play their way to
victory in battles' rages,

flowerlike grown
unhesitatingly harmonious from each root,
trusting calmly in a holy
earth beneath each foot,

whose flesh is spirit,
whose spirit is flesh –
flowerlike grown
like a strange person I met.

The Gods

The gods' chariots
do not shake the clouds,
they glide silently
forward like rays.
The gods' steps are
as hard to hear
as the grass's scarcely
perceived murmur.
Cautiously, cautiously
follow those paths
that smell of their
healing closeness.
Call no names!
They will fly, they will leave you
word-filled
in an empty world.

To Carolina Rediviva

I see a glimpse of you,
O Carolina, my friend, behind the birch's frosty twigs,
quietest light falls on my road
like sun in mist.

Stern and distinguished
you are like one whom life has given a protecting armour,
but by a sceptical mildness's light
sprinkled over –

like an old man's
smile of light, light snow and autumn-gentle irony,
thoughtfully, with warmth and wisdom underneath
and inside meek humility.

Anxiety

Deceit, deceit –
other was never my life.
All my shame,
pen, poor thing, write.
Write of roads far, far
from my truth away,
write of a wall round all that was best...
No, stay.

Threat of unfathomed darkness
fills my mind.
thunder-oppressive budding time
is still mine.
I want to be still,
wait and see a while,
wait for the sun,
softly smile.

What is happening in the darkness,
as I smile in vain?
Is my soul dying?
Will I never come home again?
God, God,
only keep secure
a glint of my intention
pure, pure!

Via Media

I once asked for joy without limits,
I once asked for sorrow, infinite as space.
I wonder if modesty grows with the years?
Fair, fair is joy, fair also is sorrow.
But fairest is to stand on pain's battlefield
with stilled mind and see that the sun is shining.

Winter Night

Sparkling creaking hard crust.
Lonely, lonely is the night sky over white roads.
I am filled with a angry thirst
for the winter sky.
Will you not soon leap up before my foot,
deep earth-cold water that sometimes chilled me,
O strong darkness that
my star conceals?

Then dizzyingly hard and pure
you will drown putrid lies as before you mercilessly did.
Where are you, bitter sea
of ice and truth?

Spellbound

When you are gone, then wildly hungers my soul.
When you are near, I yearn even so –
in despair I see,
stiffened, closed,
how empty and vain
the minute flows.

Your being's proud, royal flower-scent fine
I would secretly drink, a holy wine –
but mortally heavy I stand
as in dreams,
with thirst like Tantalus'
in clear, bright streams.

In solitude's time my tongue has burned
to tell you the beautiful things I knew and dreamed –
but in your nearness
my thought drowses, dumb.
My gate is closed,
and my heart goes numb.

The Nameless

Many things hurt that have no name.
Best to keep silent and accept all the same.

Much is secret, with danger obscure.
Best with respect and caution endure.

Best in the secret to firmly believe
And not to poke at the growing seeds.

'Here thought never went out searching.
All-mother, guide me with sure exhortation!'

Good to heed one's Mother's voice near –
wordless concern receives wordless cheer.

Pray for One Thing

Pray for one thing:
deep earnestness
– that which proved fatal to many –
But pray for one more thing more,
a thing that only the strong are granted:
taciturnity of heart.

HIDDEN LANDS
(1924)

Elemental Spirits

We, we are older than you,
you earth's children, proud and young.
Chaos' age-old voice are we,
Chaos' formless song we sing.

We, we are wind, we are water,
we are clouds in flight,
lamenting softly, lamenting shyly
far through the black late autumn night.

We, we are falsehood and play,
with tears a restless, playing call.
The moon, our lord, stands piningly pale.
King Vesäll, he attracts and bewitches us all.

Children of the earth – when the rain grows cruel,
hearths and bright homes you build.
A power you have that frightens us sore,
the hard steel in hands surely held.

Come, taste the pale enchanter's drink,
drink us out of the moon's bowl,
submerge yourselves in Chaos' formless power,
throw by the wayside your firm steel!

But to the sun in storming autumn
you build temples to shield against the night.
We seek woe like a drunken solace –
we are water, we are wind in flight!

The Thorn

Adeptly do you prick, thorn.
Well do you bite, cruel small arrows of the earth.
Slack, slow, carelessly heavy
my foot rests on the road.
Compelled harshly to tension,
when thorns sting,
my smarting foot flexes to run –
in flight onward it runs.

Summer Day

The sea rests morning-still,
never does it seem to have had storms,
like a mighty spirit
sunnily morning-still,
heavy with devotion – light
with clarity's strength.
Sharply and exactly is mirrored
the cliffs' naked precipice.
Transparently simple
lie the wide depths.
Clear-lined,
light and pure all stands,
drawn surely in airy calm,
washed in the fragrance of salt.
Clear-lined,
even and pure, with thought alone
the day strides into the sky's light,
fine as a precious stone.

The Way Home

I know a way that leads home.
It is hard to go that way.
Every traveller there grows poor
and small and ugly and grey.

I know a way that leads home.
That way is bare, pure-blown.
It is like leaning one's warm cheek
against unmerciful stone.

But he who has felt that stone
on his cheek's frozen blood,
will perceive how gentle its hardness is,
how faithful and firm and good.

And he will thank the stone
and the hardness love will he,
and praise the only battle
that was worth his victory.

To the Sea

O sea, sea,
how strong that drink you brew!
Your great cold
is holy purification clear.
Your light-embrace
is cool health for human children, for us who love healing.

For you, sea,
beaming soft, roaring hard
false, and faithful always,
are a beautiful simile for beautiful things:
for the bold heart's salt-foamed way in the world.

Guiding Principle

You my day! I do not want
to be only night, and hard dross, too –
for from your cheek spreads sweetly untouched
spring mornings' brilliance of dew.

You my sun! I do not want
to be only autumn and wind blowing cold –
for in your gaze smiled triumph-glad
blue crystal that spring skies hold.

You my peace! I do not want
to be only defiance, war's obstinacy –
for too young and budding golden
was the new life you gave to me.

The Stars

Now it is over. Now I awake.
And it is calm and easy to go,
when there is nothing left to expect
and nothing to suffer any more.

Red gold yesterday, dry leaf today.
Tomorrow nothing will be there.
But stars burn silently all around
tonight in the sky as before.

Now I want to give myself away,
so I have not a fragment left.
Say, stars, will you receive
a soul of treasures bereft?

With you is freedom without flaw
in peace of far eternities.
He never heaven empty saw
who gave you his battle and dreams.

The Unknown One

I have never seen your healing hand.
You come in the dark, when no one knows.
I wait in silence and reliance shy
in loneliness.

You my sister and mother, you and I and not I,
your name is night, an enigma's dark sun,
I sense you immense and mighty and blind
and soundlessly dumb.

You know depths of horrors I have not seen,
I tremble to break your law's secret way,
But you know a solace mild denied to me
by sunbright day.

I have silently hidden in you my wound
and ached among thorns till my soul was bare.
In the darkness you touched the bush – it leapt
into wild roses there.

Happy He That Has Gods

Happy he that has gods,
he has a home.
Solace and a sure ground
are granted only by them.

Pledge yourself as a warrior
at an altar there.
Delivered is your soul
in the hour of prayer.

Rest there awaits you
only in battle's stress.
Only between the shields
is there rest.

Compulsion to shiny weapons,
peril and faith, as well –
then will a home be raised for you,
where you can dwell.

To a Poet

You *knew*, then...!
For had you not known,
you would never have been able to say such things.

Strange twilight joy, that you also knew
all this heavy grief.
Your lost friendship wanders through centuries.
It calms fever's fire.
And when I fall asleep consoled,
it feels as though you sat by my bed, like father, and held my hand.

The Great Multitude

They have won. They rest. How their crowns shine.
Their long, long rest has no end.
They have tasted darkness. They have drunk death.
Their word was eternal: 'Amen!'
Their faithful God
in the hard night bound their garland of honour.
Its name is more than joy.
Its name is life's deep courage.

They have won. They rest. How their crowns shine.
May we endure. See, life is not long.
May we remember the rest. May we remember the crown.
May we remember the watchword.
In the safety of a barren sky
is our last dwelling prepared and our secure stronghold.
Its name is greater than joy.
Its name is life's deep courage.

Learn To Be Silent

Each night on earth is full of pain.
Heart, learn to be silent.
The hard souls, hard shields
reflect light from the home of the stars.

Your lament makes you weaker.
Heart, learn to be silent.
Only silence heals, silence hardens,
untouchedly chaste and guiltlessly true.

You seek suffering's ardent life!
Heart, learn to be silent.
By wounds and fever no one is made strong.
Bright as steel is heaven's stronghold.

The Invisible Things

I

You faithful things
that would my faith desire,
With you I forget
that I hold people dear.

You things secure.
before you I can fall in peace,
but mists and dew
are all friendship's promises.

You strong things,
that have no body and no soul,
Oh, make for me with you
the safest bed of all.

II

And yet – you, my friend,
the things you gave to me.
Your beauty, it is in them.
Else none in them would be.

You became my heavy thirst
for worlds of white relief,
You became the vision cool
that steels me to all grief.

You glimpse of distant goals,
that stretch your wing so free,
my way is a way to you.
Else none in them would be.

To Sleep

The night's baptism of the deep,
you, in whose rivers
the spirit thinks it strokes against
the sea that is called death –
it is life's sea he touches,
life's to-be-feared
beyond...

Pour your trance's riddle!
Slowly I step out
into the subterranean
misty water
that which unseen washes
the roots of our daily lives,
that which carries
of foam of our daily lives –
that from whose darkness
raised itself, woken,
too deep for what thought knows,
the body's fine, venerable,
immense, immense magnificence.

Pour your trance's riddle,
wash from my spirit
the past day's faded
dust and residue!
Death, who give life,
let me plunge again
into the light, life-renewed!

New Ways

Here new ways go.
Quietly let us fare.
Come, let us seek
a new flower, and fair.

Throw away what we possess!
Everything attained, complete
lifelessly oppresses us,
not worthy of dream, song and deed.

Life is that which awaits,
what one cannot know of, or speak...
Come, let us forget!
New things and fair let us seek!

Unscathed

Unscathed from smoke and fire
goes he that wills a work.
Listen, o spirit, adventurous one,
listen well and mark!

Wild-winged butterfly,
every bloom is yours.
Unpunished you stepped in
to death's bitter flowers,

flit childishly out of depths
where your need was most,
innocent and pure as fire
with your future-thirst.

laughing gently, gently
– for what way is worth tears? –
see life enticing
as discovery's voyage nears.

Without shame, without guilt
you weigh evil, you weigh good.
All that you sought and all that you found
were merely steps to you –

steps that led to deeds.
Listen, o my spirit, listen and mark!
Unscathed from smoke and fire
goes he that wills a work.

Spring Song

In springtime, in sprouting time,
the seed its shell destroys,
and rye becomes rye and pine becomes pine
in freedom without choice.

A thrill of voluptuousness
passes through body and soul –
that I am I, necessarily I –
a sprout that's come up whole,

a spring shoot whose growing power
I scarce envision yet –
but the stem's sap of bitter taste,
with pleasure I know it.

Then begone, all my cowardice!
To my future I belong.
I take the right to grow now
as my roots will, and as strong.

The Stars' Solace

I asked a star last night
– far away, where no one lives, a light –:
'Whom do you light, strange star?
You move so large and bright.'

It made my pity grow mute,
when she looked with her starry gaze,
'I light a night eternal,
I light a lifeless space.

My light is a flower that withers
in the skies' late autumn, rough.
That light is all my solace.
That light is solace enough.'

Evening Stillness

Feel how near Reality dwells.
She breathes near here
on evenings with no wind.
Perhaps when no one looks, she shows herself,

The sun glides over rock and grass.
In her silent play
life's spirit is concealed.
Never as this evening was he so close.

I have met a stranger with silent lips.
If I had reached out my hand
I would have brushed his soul,
as we passed each other with timid steps.

Victory

Victory, victory has no voice,
no rushing sound of delight.
Are there such simple and even roads
Under such soberly sparing light?

Victory, victory has no hue.
Against his gaze splendour seems thin.
Quiet and pale in his halo pale
he glides home out of falsehood and din.

Victory, victory is seldom seen,
moves past like a spirit-guest.
Blessed are those whom his clear form
awaits with light at death's feast.

The Child

To the rock Prometheus lay bound.
A child went out in the early morning hour.
'Stop, child, and here behold
man's friend bound in iron
for all the good he did!'
But the child, frightened
by the words' greatness, the eyes' defiance,
crept past with a prayer to Zeus
away to gentlest games. – –
I would follow you silently, where you go.
The wise and the children, they play their way to
that which in heaven is hid.

The Spring Water

A spring water is justice,
clear and colourless.
A scarce-perceptible and strange
fine taste it has.
But when wine is to be had,
such drink is so poor.
Nothing but water is the spring.
Yet I yearn for it there.

Nothing but water is justice,
nothing much to attain –
too close, hard to love,
a bitter drink to drain.
Lord, give me justice,
give my soul its peer!
Lord, give me water,
colourless and clear!

You Shall Thank

You shall thank your gods,
if they force you to go
where you have no footprints
to trust to.

You shall thank your gods,
if all shame on you they pin.
You must seek refuge
a little further in.

What the whole world condemns
sometimes manages quite well.
Outlaws were many
who gained their own soul.

He who is forced to wild wood
looks on all with new sight,
and he tastes with gratitude
life's bread and salt.

You shall thank your gods,
when your shell they break.
Reality and kernel
the sole choice you can make.

Grandfather

I have seen Grandfather in the summer night's light,
alone in the night's clover-scent.
By the well of the farm
he stood bowed,
and sharpened the harvesters' scythes.
Like a fading shadow so grey,
as old he as the farm,
he seemed yet to live as living a life as it.
His fragile song I will not forget.

'O masterful father in the farm,
to Grandfather you are nought but a boy.
I am the first who turned your earth.
When the plough strives in the furrow,
do you remember me then?
In times beyond memory
I began, from stones heaved aside,
to raise the cairn that marks the land's limit.

For a thousand years
I have built it and built with all of you who built,
held the plough's shaft with all you who ploughed.
I have a share in your work,
have a right to demand.
You know well what it is:
that the holy seed shall grow
constantly, constantly
here on those fields where I
for the first time sowed it.'

Some Hearts Are Treasures

Some hearts are treasures
that never can be done.
Their owners strew them generously
out in streams of sun.
Gratefully we take
the gift in cautious hand.
Hail and happy, blessed one,
who handles gold like sand!

Some hearts are fires
that burn deep below.
In coldest night thrown there
a reflection on the snow.
Enchanted thus, no one
in constant longing burns
as he that sees that shimmer one night
and forth to the fire yearns.

Tonight the Heaven Has No Garb

Tonight the heaven has no garb.
He shivers naked.
And never saw I yet his gaze
so all-too waking.

Say, when you fall asleep tonight:
A day is won.
On the road where one loses all
a rest's begun.

Then you will live from day to day
and lose, lose fast,
and yet desire still to remain
until the last.

Then you will find life strong,
if you can burn.
Then will each loss become a gain –
for you shall turn

ever further towards that ground of life
that gave you birth,
and beyond all dreams' deceit
the cause is there –

until in the hour of your greatest loss
your soul, burned down,
goes to the place of extinguished lights.
A day is won.

The Wanderer

Tell me, nymph from Knowledge's wells,
are there things to show to me here?
Dizziness seizes me, laughter and terror.
The air has paths that bear!

Alone with you, you eagle-eyed one,
I wander far, so far ascend,
frozen roads, chiming roads
without a goal or end.

All the holy days of love
their evening and aloneness know.
Faithful wait in the evening light
you that search and know.

All that I meet I will leave again.
Nymph, you heal burning woe.
Chiming roads, chiming roads
happy with you I will go.

Follow me hence through life's days,
teach me to say at darkness' door:
'Nothing I knew, little know I –
yet it is more than before!'

Wish

Oh let me live aright,
and rightly die some day,
so that I touch reality
in evil as in good.
And let me be still
and what I see revere.
so that this may be this
and nothing more.

If of all life's long course
a single day were left,
then I would seek the fairest
that lives on earth possess.
The fairest thing there is on earth
is only honesty,
but it alone makes life to life
and to reality.

So is the wide world
a dew-cup's petal here.
and in the bowl there rests
a drop of water clear.
That single still drop
is life's eye-apple, sure.
Oh, make me worthy to look in it!
Oh, make me pure!

To a Friend

On outspread wings in the heights the eagle sails.
The air is thin where he glides, and hard to breathe.
In the mountain winter's desolate air he is lonely far.
Twilight and cold are his retinue –
his only joy
the joy of feeling himself fly on strong wings.

How high you move in the emptiest winter skies,
brave as the eagle because of a lightning will.
You abstained from striving for happiness, you chose steep
paths that frighten us weak ones.
How pale you wander,
wander with swift and resilent steps like the wind.

My world is like yours, and yet it is not like it.
Laughing, my star dances among starry riddles.
Your iron-grey joy, I love it from far in the distance.
Let me go by your side
and reach with my gaze
into your wintry world and your lightning will!

Burning Candles

Now cries the night aloud in need,
with unknown dread a-quake.
Now light I here two candles straight
for eternal darkness' sake.

If the Lord's angels pass by here,
the light will call to them,
then they will hear the flames sing my prayer,
and bear it with them home.

They are warriors who go in armour of fire
with word from the Almighty's house.
Their speech has no words for harsh and sweet.
but for burning candles it has.

That is why they stand on the storm's back
between the whipping wings' din,
that is why they smile at the darkness's power
and meet the cold with disdain.

O Lord my God, O terrible God,
Your mantle's roar booms free.
I pray for flowers and pray for peace –
but give burning candles to me!

Songs About Fate

I

Fate is a desert.
God dwells in its sand.
If you seek your Sinai
you receive his command.

Fate is a strip of land
with many stones spread.
Happy he that endures:
he shall earn bread.

Into heaven's halls
no one goes before
he has stepped unafraid
through Fate's door.

II

You know you bear a shackle
and hear the chain rattle.
But one who hammers hard and long
Can make a shield of its metal.

You know you bear a poison.
But all death's juices
becme in a wise and careful hand
kind healing forces.

You think you bear a cross,
but it's a tool, you know.
Your life's the material. Look here, take hold,
and let the martyr go!

III

Wish for nothing that others have had:
all happens one single time.
Wish for nothing that some bard
has sung in his loveliest rhyme.

One star-bright night, when you lie awake,
Fate will knock at your door
and seek you with eyes of colour strange,
which no one spoke of before.

She fell like dew from the air,
from the bosom of space she came,
and no one, no one has met her gaze,
and no one has given her a name.

To you she has come from Nothing's land,
she has been created for you,
and no one, no one in age upon age
has kissed her lips more than you.

Æsir and Elves

I *Æsir and Elves Divide the Power*

The Æsir rode over the rainbow bridge
with frost-white weapons,
glimpsed far in the Iron Forest's darkness
the dripping monster's maw.
The swords rang and gleamed
when giants' names were heard.
The voices' echoes, the hooves' thunder
carried far into space.

The elves walked in sprouting grass
softly on supple feet.
Trees leapt into blossom when the elves stepped
lightly over twisted roots.
Earth's kingdom rejoiced,
sprouting spring came in.
the May night shone white
with elves' white skin.

Æsir and elves went to sessions
and divided the power of the earth.
The Æsir sat like hewn statues,
heavy with primeval splendour.
The elves slid like shadows
– they saunter as they will –
shadows of all that does not exist
but one day perhaps will.

Æsir and elves conferred
and divided the earth up thus:
to Æsir all that a hand can take
and all that a word can reach,
to Æsir all that is spoken
and all the time that flew –
to elves that which thereafter remains:
all that is namelessly new.

Æsir and elves conferred
and divided the family of men:
to Æsir those who hold fast

to their fathers' inherited right,
chieftain and warrior
and every sacrificial priest
and all who pray in temples –
from east and to west.

Æsir and elves conferred
and divided the race of men:
to elves those who obey blindly
a day that has not yet dawned,
all who sacrifice in the forest
and do not support the fathers' laws
and all who grow like wild trees –
all, from north to south.

Thus did they confer, and thus it was.
Thus they steer the earth's ring.
The Æsir dispose over watchwords in battle
and visible signs and things.
But the elves they control the things
that have never had a name,
and all that they have and all that they give
is the force of fertility's flame.

II *The Elf Dagur Sings About Fate*

In the world's tree nine days
sacrificed he hung
– so pale I never saw any,
god or man –
erect, with relentless mouth,
his ruler's hands clenched,
above the sacrifice he made
his eyelids closed.
But my mind
jumped like a snake – I cried: 'Who has done it?'
The dark voice answered, tremblingly low:
'I myself have done it.'

Little do I know of wisdom's well,
never yearned to be there.
Its lustre is black. I know a spring,
gleaming silver-white:

deep, deep near life's roots
a wave washes my mind.
No one demanded my eye as a pledge.
I drink freely in there.
Like a stream
flows my day – as though I had never heard
the strange answer I hear each night in my dreams:
'I myself have done it.'

Then the earth's blossoming spring seems to me
like dead things and dust
against him, sacrificed to himself
in the ash's whistling air.
Then my thought seeks in vain a well
that seems worthy of the feat.
a drink that must be cruelly won
with costly sacrifice.
No power
resembles theirs, who were silent, were silent and did it.
Through the darkness shines with splendour of flames:
'I myself have done it.'

The old witch spoke the truth.
'The strong,' she said one time,
'are born for gaze of lofty powers
and song of trembling man.
The more a strong one can suffer harm,
the more difficult things can he learn,
and dark Norns rejoice to see
how heavy a load a man can bear.'
Never yet
bore I a burden – and am not aware that I ought to.
But that dream, none is as proud as it:
'I myself have done it.'

III *Odin and Rindur*

(By means of forbidden magic Odin had won the elf-daughter Rindur, who according to the counsels of the Norns would give birth to Baldur's avenger.)

'Dark runes I carved, which no hand should carve,
I who am called chieftain in heaven's hall.
Heaven and earth are sick. Heaven and earth will break.

Myself guilt-bowed I will fall on Vigrid's slope.
Once, irrevocably, happens all that happens,
lonely, eternal, carved in stone it stands.'
   'King, one thing I know that always returns:
the earth's holy breathing, autumn and spring.'

The earth's forests murmured quietly in time's dawn,
murmur still, when the gods' power is all.
Under the spinning, under the swell of the fates
moves an engendering sea of deep crystal.
Sleep, shuttle of the Norns! Nothing is transformed.
Worlds waken in new suns' gold.'
   'Once, irrevocably, have I already acted –
yearn to pay on Vigrid's slope my debt.'

The Tree

When my door is shut and my lamp has gone out
and I sit in twilight's breathing wrapped,
then I feel around me move
branches, a tree's branches.

In my room where no one else lives
the tree spreads a shadow as soft as gauze.
It lives silent, it grows well,
it becomes what some unknown one thinks.

Some spirit-power, power secret made,
in the trees' hidden roots its will has laid.
I am frightened sometimes and ask in fear:
Are we so surely friends?

But it lives in calm and it grows still,
and I know not where it strives and whither it will.
It is sweet and bewitching to live so near
one whom one does not know...

The Shield-Maiden*

I dreamed about swords last night.
I dreamed about battle last night.
I dreamed I fought by your side
armoured and strong, last night.

Lightning flashed harsh from your hand,
and the giants fell at your feet.
Our ranks closed lightly and sang
in silent darkness' threat.

I dreamed about blood last night.
I dreamed about death last night.
I dreamed I fell by your side
with a mortal wound, last night.

You marked not at all that I fell.
Earnest was your mouth.
With steady hand the shield you held,
and went your way straight forth.

I dreamed about fire last night.
I dreamed about roses last night.
I dreamed my death was fair and good.
So did I dream last night.

---

* In Norse, *skjaldmær* (Swedish skjöldmö), an 'Amazon',
a female warrior who fought alongside men [tr.]

THE HEARTHS
(1927)

The Hearths

Dedication

Here on Uppsala's plains, remote and cold,
in the winter nights we have often strolled.
Silent we walked. The plain lay nearby.
The stars had flamed since eternity.

The stars flamed, frightening, mute,
Side by side we went, strangers, on foot,
divided in striving, divided in eye,
Dear to us both were the plain and the sky.

Once folk the ancient hearths did raise
here in the far-off worlds' shimmering gaze.
Fire against fire in time no one knows
gathered their flocks while the earth froze.

Here fields were ploughed by the first to plough,
ploughed while in forests the wolves did howl.
Here on the sacred hearths glowing red
from the corn was baked a coarse, hard bread.

Here stood the court, where crowds made sacrifice,
full of dread in the threat of a long winter's ice,
full of wailing under vaults with light a-shake,
when round earth universal night did quake.

See how the lights on the plains twinkle cold,
fighting the dark that the winter nights hold!
The night is unending, blown bark, the earth's.
Give me your hand! We're the brood of the hearths.

1

By ice-walls and ice-silence
is peace protected in my daybreak land,
where the air trembles, pale with hunger
for sun-life and sun-brand.

The thorn-thickets in fearful waiting
in hollow trunks hard round close in
all the flames that pray and beg
to soon burst forth in blossoming.

You know the word, you alone.
Speak, speak and wake my land!
Free the trees from their daybreak anguish,
light the air with your lifted hand!
Blossoms shall rain for your foot to trample,
sunbeams dance when smiles you pour.
Speak, speak! I desire to blossom
you to happiness, and nothing more.

Silent is space, pale with hunger.
Stiff and cold is my closed hand.
By ice-walls and ice-silence
is peace protected in my daybreak land.
And well I know that the magic word,
it is never said, I will never be free.
Mute your narrow lips close
when proud you stride like a deer past me.

2

The whole of my soul I have fixed to one thought,
hard, hard, so I felt it with my hand,
the whole of my soul I have hurled through the air
to you, far away,
If you see it lie like an asteroid fallen,
still after flight glowing in the sand,
if you walk past it in your vaulting rhythm.
then you are likely not thinking of me.

The whole of my soul I have fixed to a single thought,
the whole of my soul lies heavy before your feet.
I myself am so empty it hurts and aches.
You, you my friend!
Do you not notice, or will you not notice
the thing that's been torn from its trembling roots?
Have you no use for my poor soul?
Am I just in the way again?

3

If I take your wasted hand,
they will wither,
all the dreams of sunlit lands.
Let them fall!
Blossoms in white and pink,
fruit to harvest,
all is worth nothing
against your burden.

Waves with salt foam,
golden rocks
pale against your grey,
leafless evenings.
If I cannot ever
heal fate's blows –
give me your bitter day
to share!

Give me your meagre autumn!
I can freeze.
If there is a glint of consolation
it will glow.
Only a splash of light
is given to you
here in your empty house,
I give my life.

4

Each word from you is like a seed.
Its root bores deep away.
I waken from a secret pain
and find no remedy.

Consumes me then like bitter thirst
each movement that you made.
Each intonation and each glance
grows near and bright and great.

My day is grey with me and mine,
which makes my figure dull.
But mirror-bright is the night's world,
where you are all, all.

5

I think death is like you,
tall and pale and straight like you,
temples cast in a vault that is the same,
sea-eyed, distant-eyed as you
and with the same lips, closed by pain.

You are death. I am yours,
my hand yours and my mind yours.
You have deadened all life's burgeoning,
lulled into a sorrowful sleep
dream and deed that scarce have tried their wing.

But I love you, my death,
you my long, bitter death,
in whose closed hand my life withers away.
You my sweet, sweet death –
I bless your torture's every day!

6

All, all I owned
was thine more than mine.
All the most beautiful I wanted
was thine, thine, thine.

Aloud with thee I spoke
what no one in the world knows.
On endless roads
thou wast my loneliness.

If I lay awake at night
with nothing in my thought,
if I breathed, I felt thee, thee.
Thou wast round about.

Lifeless is life,
where thou dost not remain.
The world is an immense shell,
that has no kernel in.

7

Light lily bells on Kungsängen's plain
I plucked one spring, when I thought it was fall.
My heart was like them – only much less light –
a mute, red bell that begged to call.

Where goes all the song that is choked and locked in?
Where goes all the longing that attains not a thing?
Perhaps it lies mixed in the water and soil.
Perhaps is is there in the wind's whistling.

Though nothing has happened, I can manage no more.
Mortally weary am I. What have I done?
Perhaps I have striven in lands none have seen?
Hard I toiled at the gate of the rising sun!

I dragged stones in sleepless night.
Then I built a marble palace in shimmering elegance.
My anguish raised the pinnacles. Of the fountain's laugh
one hears no more that every drop was once tears.

Like fire burn the roses towards the pillars' stone,
and sunwhite towers drink blue peace that the heavens give.
But over the gate it says SOLACE. And the air is pure.
And I have prayed to the angels that there you shall live.

I put my bells by your locked, closed door.
To release their tongues was beyond my hand.
You say that your life is as bitter as before.
But I have built a palace for you in a far, far land...

8

That which is said once is always said
and till the end of time will stay,
and no night of anguish has power
to wipe that word away.

But strange it is, that a single word
can choke the beauty we recall
and turn our aery dream to earth,
till remorse alone is all.

Thus grow cool two long and heavy years,
when the fairest things budding came,
before only one word, that eternally stands
and turns my life to shame.

9

On my knees I want to give thanks
because you smiled.
Through stifling air and restlessness
moved a gentle wind, mild.
So bitterly salt are the tears
a repentant one must give.
I know you despise me.
I know you forgive.

In long days and nights
I have cruelly learned here
that we are here to lose
what we hold most dear.
Your hem I want to kiss
because you smiled.
A smile without scorn,
That is much, high-piled.

10

I feel your footsteps in the hall.
I feel in each nerve your hurried steps.
which otherwise no one will notice.
Around me sweeps a wind of fire.
I feel your footsteps, your beloved footsteps,
and my soul hurts.

You move far away in the hall,
but the air billows with your footsteps
and sings as the sea sings.
I listen, caught in your consuming force.
In the rhythm of your rhythm, in time to yours,
beats my pulse in hunger.

11

There is a happiness of death,
a happiness of destruction,
which to my thirsting mouth
only one can give,
a happiness inexorable
to senselessly embrace
and sink deep and dark
into annihilation's well.

I broke free of your shadow.
Around me it grows.
I hear your name
As I follow my ways.
I chose the light of day,
and I want your dark.
I will give sight and life
for your soul and your embrace.

12

I am victory-crowned with suffering's wreath,
with the burning flowers of new, fresh pain,
though my shame was effaced by a hand so cool,
and mercy-mild your judgement came.
I am tottering drunk with aching and woe
I have tasted the bitter drink I desire
I want more. I want to see the cup's base.
I want to die on my threshold here.

Now the night has life, now the sky has power,
now the earth and things are in reality caught.
I am blissful in the splendour of the great dark
and with living pain I am hot.
I am proud to share the sorrow that is yours,
I am rich with all the old pain you gave breath.
But that swoon of rejoicing that binds me in,
that is the breathing of death.

13

The snow it falls, the wind it whines,
frozen is Fyri's river.
The earth is lame and the heavens blind,
and life lies deserted forever.

It was a dream, a dream yesterday,
Today I have already woken.
When will your pain be again so intense
that I must share its hurting?

A day is so long. A day is so long.
Even longer is the night.
My mind is enclosed in a frozen vice,
and my thought shrinks ever more tight.

14

I want to freeze in the street here below
To see two windows in a gable glow.
To me the one who lives there is very dear.
I grow sick at heart when there's light in there.

I will go to the corner, I will slowly turn,
so I'll catch a glimpse of you maybe, then.
That you are so near...Why am I here?
I grow sick at heart when there's light in there.

15

Falling stars that the night scatters,
lightnings that glitter in flight,
proud suns that the darkness drowns –
who will call that destruction?
Tongue of fire till the last
you shall die, you shall fade,
unbending in losing all,
heavy with fate as an ancient song.

Mountain summits in immense outline,
sea's expanses at break of day,
great forests in miles-wide stretching –
such is all I know of you.
Sea-deafened in the roar of surf,
sun-dazzled in the light of snow,
lulled in triumphant dreams of murmuring pines –
thus do I bless your splendour.

I Distrust...

I believe in those who live on a farm
and break the soil.
They take their strength from nourishing earth,
and strengthen the earth as well.

I distrust those who seek in want
a distant home.
They gladden so few, and only their sort.
But I am one of them.

Sooner my starving soul, I suppose,
like a dog with no master would stray
suspiciously shy round barred-up house
and freeze pitifully away,

than be chained fast to watch its farm
in honourable calling
and raise to the homeless migrant pack
a conviction-ridden howling.

I see them move over moor and marsh
wherever the dream will fly.
I know that I am blood of their blood.
What use then am I?

In the Dark

In the dark I lie and hear
bells that outside thunder near
with long and heavy, even strokes,
like deep breaths the darkness takes.

They deaden all and make all sleep
and free each object's misty shape
in long and heavy, even boom
that thought will never be free from.

I am amongst those who scarce exist
and only know and reminisce
about old darkness's beating heart
that hopes to see no morrow start.

that fears no morrow or its start.

Compelled

Of poverty I am a priest,
and will probably always be.
Who nothing has can dare the most,
for deed and thought set free.

I hear the evil voice's scorn:
'Virtue you make of need.
What have you then to abstain from?
What if you *had* your bread?'

Yes, it is true that I have stood
and begged at happiness' door
and wept when I was given nought
and all was empty as before.

Yes, it is true that all's compelled.
But is it worth less then?
One meaning in our song is held:
to make our fate a friend.

To the Shadow of a Reality

You are one of my dreams –
good if no one wakes me! –
one of my beautiful candles,
that darkness not cover me.
Fighter for goals so pale,
ice and glass and sharpened steel!
The brilliant day
I scarce know if the dream will bear.

There is solace in the dream's perfumes,
cool, scarcely perceptible.
Yet I would give them all away
for the earthly real.
Warmth of dear beautiful hands...
I want to love, not fantasise.
Life's ripeness
the dream will never imitate.

The Two Lineages

My song is sung for the folk of Wrath
on the heath that is thistle-ridden,
for those whom the angel with flaming sword
drove out of forfeited Eden.
Thistle-down, thistle-down
over the fields wind-driven,
without the strength to root and grow
inside the pleasure garden.

But the legends say that God's sons
formerly found earth beauteous
on the hills of Morn, in the golden gleam
of primordial ages' radiance,
and the daughters of men were there as guests
in nights of the moon's billow-flounces,
sowed children from their ether-seed,
from lineage of heavenly princes.

The happy one meets their offspring,
and their hands bring happiness.
I have seen them go midst the thistles
who walked on the shores of the blest. – – –
But there is also value
in nights of sleepless dolour,
and he who knows what anguish is
knows more than many a scholar.

I have seen them walk midst the thistles.
They are free, they are weightless and clear,
and I quiver with longing and worship
for a gaze and a movement mere.
But say, who has touched our family's root,
those souls of glittering streamings
or you – with your eyes that are full of night
and your red mouth of bloodstained dreamings?

The Swallows

Hurrying, arrowing swallows, on wings resting
high in the blue expanses,
wind-light in whistling gusts
scorning the earth's inertness –
like a laugh of ridicule,
clear, light, ringing,
with contempt your flight meets our hearts' weight,
like a jubilation,
leaping from heights,
tidings of space's own
power that plays, and light can penetrate...
Sun goes down,
but up there lingers all the day's grand state,
round about you,
high in a playfully won,
airy place, happy, fortunate.

To Someone Who Is Very Young

Slender new moon,
white new moon,
pale-shimmering flame, lit
in the night's wide room,

clear blue moth,
frail blue moth,
startled awake and waiting-tensed,
when warm falls the twilight gloom,

fragile flower-bell,
bright flower-bell,
glass-brittle through and through,

elf and spring-being,
sylph and spring-being –
child, may happiness come to you!

I Want to Meet...

Armed, erect and and closed in armour
forth I came –
but of terror was the mail-coat cast,
and of shame.

I want to drop my weapons,
sword and shield.
All that hard hostility
made me cold.

I have seen the dry seeds
grow at last.
I have seen the bright green
spread out fast.

Mightier than iron
is life's tenderness,
driven forth from the earth's heart
without defence.

The spring dawns in winter's regions.
where I froze.
I want to meet life's powers
weaponless.

From a Bad Girl

I hope you're having a rotten time.
I hope you're lying awake like I am,
and feeling strangely glad and stirred
and dizzy and anxious and very disturbed.

and suddenly you'll hurry up
to settle down and sleep like a top.
I hope it takes you longer than you think...
I hope you don't even get a wink!

The stars grow in the spring...

The stars grow in the spring
great as drops that quiver,
soft as living creatures
with white bodies a-shimmer.
swelling like sacred fruits,
falling near, near,
too ripeningly heavy
for fragile heavens to bear.

Trembling starry creatures,
fair and defencelessly naked,
yearning to loosen and glide,
to touch the earth and waken,
yearning to serve their fate,
written above depth in light,
yearning to fight and create
and taste death and life.

Heaviest and whitest of all
near the horizon hangs
one that is willing to fall
ripe and clear to the hand,
Sense that the hour is near.
Someone waits for us to meet.
Man with the temper of stars,
into my womb shake a fruit!

Torkel Tyre*

East of Bjura village
is a wild and desolate stretch,
where lichen-shaggy fir trees
stand sullenly on watch.
There lived Torkel Tyre,
till murder outlawed the wretch.

Near Bjura village
lies a mossy stone.
If one hides behind it
when evening has begun,
one sees the village glimmer
with many a warm tone.

'There's a light in Halvar's farm.
There's a light in Torsten's place.
There sits Torsten carving
by a crackling log fire blaze.
There's a light in Kettil's cottage.
Each light I recognise.

What did I know of land,
safe on land ensconced?
Now on long nights I stand
and count the treasure I lost.
Gold gleams above the drifts
in winter nights' blue dust.'

Thus stood he and looked and looked,
when the sliding of skis was heard.
A panting maiden came wild in flight,
to the village in need she was turned.
Close behind her a shadow slid
with eyes that burned.

But Torkel seized his knife.
He hewed, he stabbed, he cut,
and sharp, white teeth
gave answers obstinate.
Near morning he felled the wolf,
but tired to death, lay flat.

We found him where he lay.
And note that we acted well.
We sent word to the priest.
He delivered the man's soul.
When the sun rose over the forest,
we beat Torkel to hell.

We could have spared his life,
but the value of such is not great.
A murderer was Torkel.
We acted as we ought.
We all are men from the land,
and this was done aright.

* 'Tyre' (Icelandic 'tyra'): the name means 'lamp' [tr.].

The Carillon

'The carillon plays, and the town listens quiet.
Such silver-pure sounds our world has never heard.
Such beautiful playing has no one, so elaborate no one.
O master, divine one, you, a miracle you have worked!'

'A man works no miracle, but God, God alone.
A man works no miracle, but God with his hand.
As dust are our lives, and our deaths a shadow's shadow.
Only he deserves reverence here in earthly life's land.'

Then spoke the town's prince: 'My carillon is glorious.
With honour does the town raise its summits to the skies.
That never you may lend your art to another,
as pledge, O master, I demand your eyes.' –

'My hand was made to work, my spirit to create,
for a hundred more carillons to life I was waked.
See here! My eye gleams with the fire from above,
which no prince may light, if once it is slaked.'

'There awaits all you wish for, that men can give you
of carefree days at my covered board
– cruel was I never –, only not the hours of toil.
Be pleased with your fate – know, I stand by my word.' –

'I suppose, mild prince, I must try your mildness.
I bow to the power of your princely discretion.
But one more time let me see my work and rejoice!
O powerful, o mild one, grant my plea satisfaction!'

Up he stepped to the bell-tower, and down again,
and the executioner took his eyes, then he led him away.
In his pain he was mute; but more mute his bells.
And never again did the carillon play.

Then said the town's prince: 'You shall die for your misdeed,
you thief, who stole from the town its voice's fair laud.
On thousands your wretched eyes, your pride you've avenged...'
He said: 'May I die! I have avenged God.'

The Condemned

When the great trial reached its end,
after judgement, speeches, all
the silent thoughts of the condemned
held colloquy in the silent hall.

One man to the other said:
'No one knows how we shall fare.
Perhaps it is really just the start
of a work that awaits us there.

Your features are very pale,
white as that white glow,
living as flames live.
To death we've still far to go.

Burning and without fear
we shall go to the bitter last,
burning and without fear
our spirits will rise like a spark.

Through empty, cold expanses
the wind may drive it far,
but where the forest is driest,
two hot sparks will fall.'

The Man Without Mercy

He is the man without mercy –
eyes of shimmering amber,
eyes of shining cold gold,
hands of ivory bone:
clear and hard eyes,
fine and hard hands –
reckoned by passionate dreamers
as stone of the desert's stone.

The desert has wide realms of sand
and strange springs,
dead cities and living leaves
and light for an anchorite.
There he has pitched his camp,
his thin, needy tent –
Trappist in science,
an ascetic of the spirit.

His aspiring vulnerability
like a hindrance he breaks in the battle,
reckless, when needs be, and cold
to whistling, laughter, applause.
Inhuman he seems.
Like the north wind his pathos chills.
He fights the frightening fight of thought,
the man with no mercy at all.

Samson sings as he grasps the pillars of the temple:

Ordained a nazir to the Lord
you scarcely possess a name,
chosen, lifted
from the earth's mild embrace you came.
Ordained a nazir to the Lord
you are called the Lord's hand
and brandish the Lord's lightning
in terror-stricken lands.

Ordained a nazir to the Lord
the Lord's spirit you bear
and have not your own spirit
to love a mortal dear.
Woe to that hour
when man and god I failed,
when I became the man Samson,
and the order's strength quailed.

In remorse grew my power
near the millstones' din.
Of victories easily won
they spoke to Judah's son.
Now I pull down Dagon's temple,
for Samson is devoured,
and I am again a nameless one,
whose name is the Lord's sword!

The Star

Sparklingly frosty
with frozen light
the Milky Way's waves wash
stars like gravel tight.
One only is mine.
She is known to my thought –
my fate's light of eternity,
my life and my lot.

In immense strength she rose,
when dark me did cloak.
When defenceless I fell, me
to star-life she woke.
With silver nails my soul
to a star was bound.
Thus wanders free its given way
my being's kernel and ground.

Who intends to choose me
must woo the star.
In her dwells my worth,
my will in her.
In her is my home,
From her my law on high.
O star, o my deed
and my goal, you are I!

The Grass's Song

Yesterday I lay broken
in the rainshowers' stream.
Now washed and clean I rise
from degradation's dream.
I read in the light,
I hear with dread life's
eternal commandment 'Forget!'
in the morning's hum.

I saw lightnings splinter
the noblest oak,
and I saw mountains weather
in the ages' joke,
but stronger than either
from the winters' peril
in a thousand springs I rise aloft,
immortal and weak.

My root is fixed in death,
in mouldered things' dwelling-place.
I do not remember their fates,
but I feel them sprout, increase.
The past's spirit trembles
in bright green meshes
and ripens to an eternal now
in the grassy ground's peace.

The Sea

Salt, bitter salt
is the sea, and clear and cold.
In the depths much moulders away,
but the sea cleanses all.
Wild, prey-beast wild
is the surf's glittering leap,
but no human thoughts
are high as the song of the deep.
Strong, eternal and strong
is the waves' immense train,
and strong with the eternal sea
each wave soft, transient.
Though the sea asks blood of her man,
give your life to the sea.
At last, deep in the depths,
none attains a rest like he.

On the Move

The sated day is never first.
The best day is a day of thirst.

Yes, there is goal and meaning in our path –
but it's the way that is the labour's worth.

The best goal is a night-long rest,
fire lit, and bread broken in haste.

In places where one sleeps but once,
sleep is secure, dreams full of songs.

Strike camp, strike camp! The new day shows its light.
Our great adventure has no end in sight.

Of Those Who Fell Too Soon

Happy he that marches
in light of waiting's dawn.
Happy he that falls
long ere victory was won.

Before the battling army grows a host,
beings of light with mighty weapons to ply:
all the faithful who fell ere the harvest was ripened,
all the young who never had time to fade to ash.

Happy he that exchanges
the narrow life he bore
for their empire
and their victorious power.

Like pillars supporting a bridge over the deeps,
freed from human limits by human longing,
they bear on their shoulders the weary who succumb,
lead with arms of security the weak who hesitate.

Happy he that falls
and lives none the less.
In souls his soul he makes
a thousandfold increase.

Rest and death never had a portion in the strong.
They are still here in our battle. Forever they are ours.
High above the hosts their lances flame like fire,
raised as promises and signs and banners to follow.

Happy we that follow
Happy we for their giving.
We are dust and soil
and they the living.

The Falling Morning Star

'Fall,' said the Lord, 'fall,
defiant morning star!
darkness will I grant you gladly.
You are dearest to me in all the world.'

'Fall,' said the Lord, 'fall,
burning blue flame!
Gleam in the torment of the deep,
build yourself a city of black crystal!'

'Fall,' said the Lord, 'fall!
You who would taste all evil,
will you come back soon?
You are nearest to me in all the world.'

The world is dreamt...

The world is dreamt by a sleeping god,
and the dawn's shiverings moiré his soul.
The memories of things that happened yesterday,
before the world was there,
haunt, glint.
That in whose being we have no part
meets us where the way bends,
it breathes a horror that is not ours,
from the limits far away,
from worlds with other laws.
Sleep, sleep heavier, slumberer,
until the dream torments you no more,
or waken to the day, creator,
and make us real!

The World's Heart

Say, where does the world's heart burn,
the world's heart of fire?
It lives on coarse, heavy prehistoric coal:
black darkness, dense night, Chaos.
Seek there!
For thus is the nature of fire:
strong with its foe's struggle –
itself a struggle, glowing struggle –
has no other nature.
And the victory? When the darkness has disappeared in flames?
Is the victory death?
Empty question and empty fear!
The world's heart is fire,
and fire wants to conquer.

The Corrupter

I am led by a snake's gaze, rigid, cruel –
it stares towards me from the farthest distance,
guides my steps in the nearest nearness,
holds me captive in coercive fear,
binds my will...

Who gave the snake his fearful beauty,
the abyss attraction,
death sweetness?
Who gave horror the fatal delight
that entices like a darker happiness?

Perhaps there yonder, by the eternal springs,
where the veils fall,
the Corrupter will meet me in another form.
Art thou God's shadow, evil one?
God's nocturnal twin brother?

The Stones

God had given us heavy souls of stone.
Then we stood on the shore of the sea,
where the sunbeams leapt, where the foam danced, where the gulls
    sailed in light.
Then we hurled the stones in a game of dying. One must do
    something with stones.

They grazed the surface, they bounded in arcs, they glided over
    the deep like winds!

And happy is our sleep: it is touched by wings, by swallows that
    hurtle over the water.

We Sleepy Children

In by the darkened shore glides a lonely white sail,
like a tired, probing bird seeking a refuge for the night,
and above in the deepening sky a bright twilight cloud,
drifting apathetically like one who is just about to fall asleep...

Now we turn back, we sleepy children, to our home near here,
and smooth our thoughts from our brow, and smooth our deeds
    from our hands.
We leave them to fade like forgotten games, we drop them for that
    which is real
and lean with the blind trust of children against an unknown
    mother's knee.

The Bygone Days

When an old man lies ill, all his bygone days come
and sit gently in a ring around his bed.
They don't complain, they do not cry or sob.
They nod slowly and think of old things.
And each of them tells his never forgotten story,
and each of them has a candle and lights it quietly.
They are reflected clearly in the dark rivers' water.
He goes, goes beneath vaults, beneath arches of quivering light.

The Water Babies

Around our cradle billowed soft as seaweed
transparent water-sprites, intangible.
Timelessly happy we rested in windless depth.

Who tore us loose from our home?
Like eddying bubbles we sighed towards the light,
like gleaming silver fishes we glided in lead-grey sea.
Then we stood with dripping hair on the shore one morning
in an alien land.

Never will we find our way home.
We go forth as in a dream.
Our moist, dark eyes are shy of the sun.
Our cool and gentle hands are shy of action.
Our floating, yielding souls are shy of loving.
They wriggle like serpents away from all scorching heat...

We go as in a dream, our world is foam.
Our distant coolness is a greeting from our father's kingdom,
where the gates arch up from glass-green water – the gates to
      eternal rest.

Lilith's Song

The clouds hang heavy,
ripen in tepid darkness, where they're concealed,
night-blue clusters of grapes,
heavy with wine that silent pours on every field,
heavy with wine of the Deep,
heavy with secret power,
sucked out of sea and sky
and bitter dew in outermost darkness's shore.

Life's hot vapour
condenses in drops, falls in dead silent night.
Raise the cup! You shall capture
the key where no one his foot has set –
the land where the spirit freed
beyond time's border fence
tastes in eternities
things that are never felt or seen or sensed.

Behind waking worlds
see the alien seas of delight and woe
the world-deep's smithy-forges,
from which leapt like a spark what our eyes know.
Do you dare take the way there,
blazed in horror's drunkenness?
Terror-struck, blessed
you will attain the eternal Mothers' dark houses...

Blown seed on wide waters,
flower of the Deep, that never saw its root,
dragonfly shy of the night –
one day the Mothers' night will greet your foot!
Death with pain is black.
Death with joy is white.
Plunged in his murmuring waves
you will forget life's coast of clouded light.

FOR THE TREE'S SAKE
(1935)

Nowhere

I am sick with poison. I am sick with a thirst
for which nature has not created any drink.

From every field leap streams and springs.
I stoop down and drink from the earth's veins
its sacrament.

And the heavens overflow with holy rivers.
I stretch up and feel my lips wet
with white ecstasies.

But nowhere, nowhere...

I am sick with poison. I am sick with a thirst
for which nature has created no drink.

Walpurgis Night

At last I stand near the mountain of the fates.
All around like stormclouds
crowd formless beings, creatures of the twilight,
black-winged,
phosphorous-eyed.
Shall I stay? Shall I go? The road lies dark.
If I stay peacefully here at the foot of the mountain,
then no one will touch me.
Calmly I can see their struggle like a play of the mist in the air,
myself merely a lost eye.
But if I go, if I go, then I shall know nothing more.
For the one who takes those steps
life becomes legend.

Myself fire
I shall ride on coiling snakes of fire.
Myself wind
I shall fly on winged wind-dragons.

Myself nothing,
myself lost in the storm
I shall fling myself forth dead or living, a fate future-heavy.

You Call for People

You call for people of great stature. What gives great stature to a
    person?
To become nothing and forget oneself for that which is greater
    than her.

The unrepentant call out. They themselves would grow into giants
the moment they bowed their knees in the shadow of the immense
    things.

But raise your voices until the gods awake, until new gods rise up
    and answer!
When no one asks for people any more, then your people will be
    here.

Cherub

Also you, who suffer the agonies of everyone's condemnation,
also you are called to your place among the cherubim –
with lion's feet, with wings of sun,
with venerable human head:
beast-angel.
They call after you: 'Impure, impure!'
Because they were never afflicted by purity.
Flame, gather your sparks out of the corners,
the forge awaits, and the hammer that welds you to lightning
will teach you the lightning's swift purity
and your name among the cherubim.

That Hour

No breathless summer night sky
reaches so far into eternity,
no lake, when the mists lighten,
mirrors such stillness
as that hour –

when loneliness's limits are effaced
and the eyes become transparent
and the voices become simple as winds
and there is nothing more to hide.
How can I now be afraid?
I shall never lose you.

The Night's Deep Violoncello

The night's deep violoncello
hurls its dark rejoicing out across the expanses.
The hazy images of things dissolve their form
        in floods of cosmic light.
Swells, glowing long,
wash in wave upon wave through night-blue eternity.
You! You! You!
Transfigured weightless matter, rhythm's blossoming foam,
soaring, dizzying dream of dreams,
              blindingly white!
I am a gull, and on resting, outstretched wings
I drink sea-salt bliss
            far to the east of all I know,
            far to the west of all want,
and brush against the world's heart –
blindingly white!

Yes, of course it hurts

Yes, of course it hurts when buds are breaking.
Why else would the springtime falter?
Why would all our ardent longing
bind itself in frozen, bitter pallor?
After all, the bud was covered all the winter.
What new thing is it that bursts and wears?
Yes, of course it hurts when buds are breaking,
hurts for that which grows
                      and that which bars.

Yes, it is hard when drops are falling.
Trembling with fear, and heavy hanging,
cleaving to the twig, and swelling, sliding –
weight draws them down, though they go on clinging.
Hard to be uncertain, afraid and divided,
hard to feel the depths attract and call,
yet sit fast and merely tremble –
hard to want to stay
                      and want to fall.

Then, when things are worst and nothing helps
the tree's buds break as in rejoicing,
then, when no fear holds back any longer,
down in glitter go the twig's drops plunging,
forget that they were frightened by the new,
forget their fear before the flight unfurled –
feel for a second their greatest safety,
rest in that trust
                      that creates the world.

A Stillness Expanded

A stillness expanded, soft as sunny winter forests.
How did my will grow sure and my way obedient to me?
I carried in my hand an etched bowl of ringing glass.

Then my foot became so cautious and will not stumble.
Then my hand became so careful and will not tremble.
Then I was flooded over and carried by the strength from fragile
      things.

You Are the Seed

You are the seed and I your soil.
You lie in me and grow.
You are the child expected.
I am your mother now.

Earth, give your warmth!
Blood, give your sap!
An unknown power requires today
all the life I have had.

The flowing warm wave
knows no dam on earth,
wider it wants to create,
breaks its way forth.

That is why it hurts to the living quick
inside me now:
something is growing and breaking me –
my love, it is you!

If I Could Follow You

If I could follow you far away,
further than everything you know,
out to the world-loneliness
of the outermost regions go,
where the Milky Way rolls
a bright dead foam
and where in dizzying space
you seek a home.

I know: it is impossible.

But when from your baptism
shivering blind you rise,
all throughout space
I shall hear your cries,
be new warmth for you,
be a new embrace,
be close to you in a different world
among things with unborn names.

Blonde Morning

Blonde morning, lay your soft, smooth hair
against my cheek and breathe undisturbed in your silence.
The earth opens wide and wider your giant chalice,
born anew in closed darkness.
On bright wings
the Miracle lands like an immense insect
to lightly graze against unsuspecting
awakening pistils.

Morning on the seventh day...

Ripe as a Fruit

Ripe as a fruit the world lies in my lap,
it ripened last night,
and its rind is the thin blue membrane that stretches bubble-round,
and its juice is the sweet and fragrant, streaming, burning torrent
    of sunlight.

And out into the transparent universe I leap like a swimmer,
submerged in a baptism of ripeness and born to a power of ripeness.
Consecrated to action,
light as a burst of laughter
I cleave a golden sea of honey that desires my hungry hands.

Farewell

I would like to have woken you to a nakedness like a naked evening
    in early spring,
when the stars brim over
and the earth burns beneath melting snow,
I would like to have seen you just once
sink in the darkness of creative chaos,
would like to have seen your eyes like wide-open space,
ready to be filled,
would like to have seen your hands like flowers unfolded,
empty, new, in expectancy.

You are going, and nothing of this have I given you.
I never reached to where your being lies bare.
You are going, and nothing of me are you taking with you –
leaving me to defeat.

Another farewell I remember:
we were hurled from the crucible like a single being,
and when we parted, we no longer knew
which was I and which was you...

But you – like a bowl made of glass you have left my hand,
as finished as only a dead thing is and as changeable,
as without any memories other than the light imprints of fingers
that are washed away in water.

I would like to have woken you to a formlessness like a formless
        flickering flame
that finds at last its living form, its own...
Defeat, oh, defeat!

Now I Know

Now I know how much you hid and kept silent about.
That was your shell.
But why have you hidden yourself so well from me?
The thought grinds still.

I know. I remember: one single case,
where judgement was mine to wield –
and then your inner world's enchanted land
was forever concealed.

As long as our love has one chance left,
if even only one,
that long will our love be a closed hand –
and to us justice be done.

My Skin Is Full of Butterflies

My skin is full of butterflies, of fluttering wings –
they flutter out across the meadows and enjoy their honey
and flutter home and die in sad small spasms,
and not a grain of pollen is disturbed by light feet.
For them the sun exists, the hot, immeasurable, older than the ages...

But under skin and blood and inside the marrow
heavily heavily imprisoned sea-eagles move,
broad-winged, that never let go of their prey.
How would your tumult be in the sea's spring storm?
How would be your cry, when the sun annealed yellow eyes?
Closed is the cave! Closed is the cave!
And between the claws twist white as cellar sprouts
the nerves of my innermost being.

The Tree Beneath the Earth

There grows a tree beneath the earth;
a mirage pursues me,
a song of living glass, of burning silver.
Like darkness before light
must all weight melt,
where only one drop falls of the song from the leaves.

An anguish pursues me.
It oozes out of the earth.
There a tree suffers deeply in heavy layers of earth.
Oh, wind! Sunlight!
Feel that agony:
the promise of fragrance of paradise miracles.

Where do you walk, feet, that tread
so soft or hard
that the crust cracks and yields up its prey?
For the tree's sake, have mercy!
For the tree's sake, have mercy!
For the tree's sake I call you from the four points of the compass!

Or must we wait for a god – and which one?

Our Eyes Are Our Fate

Our eyes are our fate.
So lonely you become, poor eyes,
with stars that refuse to have mercy
in a living, earthly way.
Had I seen less,
I would think other thoughts,
and an outcast grows slack,
abandoned to the just.

Holy, holy, holy
is the truth, the terrifying,
I know it, I bow down,
and it has a right to everthing.
But flesh and blood shiver,
the living seeks life,
and warm is humans' company
and cold their contempt.

And praying I wander
among freezing light-years,
seeking for help
ro rise from my grave.
Remember with ardent tenderness
eyes far away,
also those that are lost
in the sea of loneliness.

Then I cannot complain.
Then I must give thanks.
With them I have shared
what I know, what I remember.
And through the darkness I sense
home and company.
Beloved sister eyes!
You existed. You exist.

Confession

Never meant to be a rebel,
and yet it was forced on me.
Why is my fate not private?
Why can I not let it be?
Or, if now I must fight,
why is there torment there?
Why not with sounding music,
when at last I am forced to dare?

Blood of my blood, that judged me harshly
and cast me out into shame,
I knew when I was ejected,
that I broke on a whole all the same,
felt a sacred communion
behind the condemning words,
knew with anguish: *you are I* –
and was bowed down to the earth.

But as I lay and believed myself mute,
I heard the darkness whine.
Souls from the same torments' room
were breathing by my side.
I heard my own cry for help
rise up from deserts void,
knew with dread: *I am you* –
and could not be quiet.

Cowardly, cowardly, thrice cowardly,
All the same, I must fight,
be struck to the ground and rise again
with all my nerves snapped.
must feel like branding irons
the judgements of the stark –
and obey and obey a scorching fire
that blossoms out of the dark.

Prayer to the Sun

Merciless one with eyes that have never seen the dark!
Liberator who with golden hammers breaks blocks of ice!
Save me.

Straight as thin lines the flowers' stems are sucked into the heights:
nearer to you will their calyxes tremble.
The trees hurl their strength like pillars towards their glory:
only up there
do they spread out their light-thirsty leaf-arms, devoted.
Man you drew
from an earth-fixed stone with blind gazes
to a walking swaying plant with heaven's wind about his forehead.
Yours is stalk and stem. Yours is my backbone.

Save it.
Not my life. Not my skin.
Over the outer no gods dispose.
With extinguished eyes and broken limbs
he is yours, who lived erect,
and with the one who dies erect
you are there, when darkness swallows darkness.
The rumbling rises. The night swells.
Life shimmers so deeply precious.
Save, save, seeing god,
what you gave.

Young Wills Whine

Young wills whine
like masterless spears.
Fear has hurled them
into space's spheres.
Trembling with battle
and strength in surfeit
they seek targets to strike
they seek powers to worship.

But wills that ripen,
they become trees and strike root,
ready to shield
a land at your foot,
a small stretch of ground,
but necessary, like life,
where something precious grows,
torn by the winds' strife.

If the glade seems narrow
against space without end
and the tree perhaps lifeless
against spears that blind,
then forget not the leaf
with its life-green colour,
and forget not the sap
that seethes through the marrow.

Be not afraid, be still
that harvest night,
when the voices say:
'Your bounds are set.
You too shall be silent
among the watching faithful.
You also shall strike root,
and become tree, and ripen.'

The Doorway

Too many times have I passed through the doorway.

It rises so high and is erased in sunlight,
and under the arch one hears passing
eternal winds in eternal spaces.
The threshold is made of promise-stones, the staircase to an altar,
to which he slips through who consecrates himself to a gift
with his past time and his time to come
and a will that is whole.

Too many times have I passed through the doorway.

And yet I pray:

Watchman at the door, lord of all beginning,
let me through! I still have strength.
As truly as I never hid anything away,
take, but take to the last fragment.
The day I divide, the day I reckon,
bar my way and cast me into the melting-furnace.
All is a door. All is a beginning.
The axle of life is in your hands.
Whole I pass under the dizzying arch,
and eternal winds in eternal spaces
drink my gift.

Idyll

Your voice and your footsteps fall soft as dew on my working day.
Where I sit there is spring in the air around me from your living
    warmth.
You flower in my thought, you flower in my blood, and I wonder
    only
that my happy hands do not blossom into heavy roses.

Now the space of the everyday closes around us two, like a soft,
    gentle mist.
Are you afraid of becoming a prisoner, are you afraid of drowning
    in the greyness?
Do not be afraid: in the everyday's innermost depth,
in the heart of all life,
there burns with quietly humming flames a deep, secret festival.

For the Hour of Great Humiliation

For the hour of great humiliation I would also give thanks,
the hour when one sees that one is naked
and without a muddying vestige of pride
lets oneself be arranged
like a speck of dust in the gleam from wondrous worlds –
wondrous everything, wondrous health and life,
wondrous shelter, bread and water,
and more than anything wondrous the undeserved favour
of a human being's eternally established trust.

Pyre

Transparent, bright and ardent,
beautiful mantle, flare,
slip your way close as water
round my body, waiting here.
I stand bound and quiet,
have no unshed defiance.

Have no resistance left,
no futile strugglings.
Thus in anguish without air
comes the peace that waiting brings.
Here all hope is laid over,
wants nothing other.

Like an aspen leaf my body,
my soul like a flickering flame,
and there far away inside
I am free all the same.
Great silence moves me
beyond all that destroys me.

Invulnerable

Invulnerable, invulnerable
is he that grasps the primordial saying:
There is no happiness and unhappiness.
There is only life and death.

And when you have learnt it and ceased to chase the wind
and when you have learnt it and ceased to be frightened by the gale
then come back and teach me one more time:
There is no happiness and unhappiness.
There is only life and death.

I began to repeat it when my will was born,
and will cease to repeat it when my will has ceased to be.
The secret of the primordial sayings
we acquire until our death.

Knowledge

All the cautious ones with long nets
meet with the sea's giant laughter.
Friends, what do you seek on the shore?
Knowledge can never be captured,
can never be owned.

But if, straight as a drop,
you fall into the sea to dissolve,
ready for any transformation –
then you will awake with mother-of-pearl skin
and green eyes
on meadows where the sea's horses graze
and be knowledge.

Dwarf Pine

Here in eternal gales
dwarf pine works its way up from the stone,
bends wearily,
knots itself defiantly,
creeps subdued.

Black against the evening's stormy sky
twisted ghostly outlines are drawn.
Monster is seized by loathing
for monster.
A groaning passes through the torn crowns:
Oh, to look one single time
straight towards the light,
to rise, a royal oak,
a boyish birch,
a golden virgin maple.

Hide your dreams, cripple.
Here are the outermost skerries. As far as the eye can see:
dwarf pine.

The Mouths

Around me float terrible mouths.
The suburban train is thudding.

These are mothers.
Mouths of predatory fish,
locked and tensed in greedy fear:
to eat or be eaten.
Themselves eaten away (no one has noticed)
they lug their entrails in string bags.
Dead eyes, dead fear,
mouths of predatory fish.

This is the lover.
Paint-swollen mushroom mouth
sucks for prey.
The shame of having given herself, the shame of the cheated
sucks for revenge of a thousand triumphs,
is never sated,
settles in layers of tortured impudence
around a wet mushroom mouth.

This is the pious man,
who with holy pursing
hides and denies his lips.
They cannot be seen, do not exist –
God himself cannot see them.
Why is he afraid of his lips?
What do they look like when he is asleep?

This is the happy woman,
she who became a possessor.
Among all those who struggle
she is the one who prevailed.
No lever will ever force open those jaws,
screwed tight around life's prize.

But over there by the window,
half-open,
flowers a mouth that captures nothing.
What do you breathe over the wide world,
so world-estranged?
Yourself?

When will you be scared down there into the deep
to predatory fish
and sucking mouths,
snatch wildly after hunted prey,
slash desperately at the others?
Tomorrow,
if you want to live.

So I will take my staff and wander
and seek another world for you,
a world where mouths are allowed to be flowers

and breathe like flowers
their life's breath
and flow like flowers
from deep sources
and stand like flowers
happily open.

Around you snap our deep-sea mouths.
The suburban train is thudding.

Sea Prayer

Sea swell, come washing,
let me taste that sound's round, salty flow,
the sound that was given me
as primordial name aeons and aeons ago!
Words that no mortal
lips can tell
lie hidden
in the fresh, cold swell.

Long, too long
I starved on human words too easily told.
I want to rise up,
I want to satisfy my mouth at my mother's board.
Like a child in loathing's remorse
lost far away to roam,
I turn hungrily round
to the songs of my home.

Let me drink
the speech of speech from a dull roar that never abates.
Let me clear
to your resting depth of light that creates.
Within soul and spirit
I hear your song.
Rise in my blood, and flower
in my tongue!

The Way Is Narrow

The way is narrow that two must go,
inhumanly narrow, it can seem sometimes,
and yet it is a human way, even so.

From buried things' primordial slime
rise monsters woken by the warmth,
and bar the way where you would climb.

No flight can make you free at last.
They appear again by new waysides.
You have no choice. You must go past.

– – – – – – – – – – – – – – – – –

The way is steep that two must go,
a way of degradation, it can seem sometimes,
and yet is a way of victory, even so.

Lonely path goes round in rings,
the same mirage in the same sand,
the same thirst for far-off things.

For two that strive, one gain know I,
more solid, heavier than the hermit's dreams:
the difficult growth to reality,

yes, all the way in to the innermost core,
where the person grows out of splintered nerves
and becomes a root and a mountain there.

– – – – – – – – – – – – – – – – –

The way is long that two must go,
a lost way, it can seem sometimes,
and yet has its goals and signposts, even so.

Has its angels, in lightning dressed.
They touch our dust with burning hand,
and heavy chains become breezes and mist.

With burning feet they touch earth's floor,
and create it anew in the morning glow
and full of health and solace and cure

and full of power over approaching fate
and intimate light, that two acquire.

The Wanderer in the Desert

You weigh with false balances
and measure with false gauges,
not before the qadi, who judges criminals,
but before Allah, Allah, blessed be his name,
he who has created life.

A thousand dates you buy for one small pearl,
but I, who hungered in the desert,
am weary of my pearl-sewn belt,
that gives no nourishment,
and I, who pined away in the sand,
will not recover the splendour in my dagger hilt,
decked with jewels
that slake no thirst.

Still in this city of minarets, far from the desert,
I will bow not before those proud portals,
those golden gates,
but before those lowly, those out-of-the-way wells
to where dusty herdsmen lead their herds,
when they bring milk in the evenings.

Your Warmth

Your warmth, your tender warmth
I ask to share,
that streamed long before man
on earth was there.
In the deep primordial forest's
downy bird's nest
that same protective warmth bore
life's founding rest.

From anguish-burning heavens
we sink down where
in the nest's darkness, life
asks nothing more.
For the clouds' games are a mirage
and mirror spray,
but all that is born and bears
is what depths give away.

Day dawns, and the skies resound
with rushing of wings.
The soaring bird rejoices:
On light I live! he sings
But hidden in the silence rests
his weal and woe.
Your warmth, your deep warmth
gives me a soul.

Legend

Over the city's sighing towers
sank all the earth's distress:
fire, plague and hunger,
war and sudden, cruel death.

The people thronged in the churches,
bowed their knees in fear,
heard the priests pray to God
for strength his penance to bear.

The mothers by the well
despaired, and help they missed.
'For the children's sake, for the children
mercy must exist.

Though in sin they were born,
to us they are very dear,
they are much dearer to us
than heaven's glory in there.'

A white-haired stranger,
one step before the rest,
beckoned them to follow,
began to wander thence.

Swarming out through the gates
more and more followed on.
In the city's midst stood a house.
A staircase there led down.

Hard-trodden floor of earth,
stool and wooden bowl.
Clad in a cloak of hair
a man knelt in that hole.

Humble veneration
burned in every gaze:
'The city is wealthy yet!
Here a holy man lives and prays.

There in intercession
his face is upward-turned;
the marks in his careworn features
by our sins have there been burned.'

Bitterly the old one laughed.
'What is it you behold?
A great, holy love,
and beyond that, nothing more?

A face's open bowl
of patience, blessed, sane,
that rises up in hunger
towards the flood of pain –

an ardent spirit's chalice
of bleeding rubies that shine,
waiting here devoutly
for the Lord's wrath's wine –

a desire to suffer
the beloved's worst punishment – –
and does no one see the lightning
down from heaven sent?

The city gave an echo
and in the same sound shook,
when he, the man strong in prayer,
his lord subdued.

Pull up all the poppies
that ask for springtimes of pain!
Cut down all the black trees
that yearn to bear tears' rain!'

Then from the crowd there stepped
a man full of fiery dread,
felled the old one to the ground –
she fell and there lay dead.

They crossed themselves, they crept away,
the daughters and sons of men.
And up to heaven's angry vault
the holy man's prayers rose again.

Eternity

An eternity long
our summer was then.
We roamed in sunny days
that had no end.
We sank in fragrant green
depths without floor
and felt no fear
of eventide's hour.

Where did our eternity go?
How did we forget
its holy secret?
Our day became too short.
In strife we form,
In spasm we rhyme
a work that shall be eternal –
and its essence is time.

But still timeless drops
fall into our arms
at a time when we're absent
from goals and names,
when the sun falls silent
over straws there alone,
and all our striving seems to us
like a game and a loan.

Then we sense that condition
we once received:
to burn in the moment
that living bequeathed,
and forget the temporal
that lasts and endures,
for creation's second,
that no gauge ever nears.

Fragment of Alcman

Sweetly singing maidens, my limbs can no longer
carry me – o would, would that I were merely the kingfisher,
when, carried across the foam of the waves by the halcyons,
he soars with sorrowless heart, the sea-dark, sacred bird!

NOTE. *The ageing chorus leader alludes to the legend that the kingfisher, when he grows old, is carried by the females, the halcyons.*

THE SEVEN DEADLY SINS
& OTHER POSTHUMOUS POEMS
(1941)

THE SEVEN DEADLY SINS
Fragment from a Cantata

Scene: Before God's Throne

Introduction

CHORUS I
> How long, how long, how long?
> Destroy us! Destroy us!

CHORUS II
> A little time, a little time, a little time!
> Have mercy!
> Have mercy!

THE ACCUSER (*recitative*)
> It is time to speak. It is truly time to speak.

CHORUS II
> Have mercy!

CHORUS I
> Destroy us!

THE ACCUSER (*recitative*)
> Out of the darkness I rise before your throne,
> I, the Accuser.
>
> From generation to generation we saved our folly's hope.
> As a newly conceived child lies hidden and is scarcely there,
> so you lay hidden in our inner being, O great folly.
> From generation to generation we were ready to deny what we
>   heard and saw.
> Who wants to be the evil thing? Who wants to be what man
>   really is?
> From generation to generation we were nothing but our secret folly,
>   our unborn one.
>
> O Lord, how near you are to that which does not exist!
> But look after us! We cannot endure any longer.
> Destroy the evil that does not care to deny itself.
> Destroy our folly's dream that is not able to make itself real.
> Destroy us.

CHORUS I
>   How long, how long, how long?
>   Destroy us!
>   Destroy us!

CHORUS I
>   We are your flock,
>   Lord, whom you failed –
>   Have trust! was your command –
>   and worse we fared.
>   From evil's mists
>   no light rose aloft,
>   out of the thunder
>   no murmur soft.
>
>   We quaked in the desert
>   abandoned, alone
>   with harsh commandments
>   written in stone.
>   They became our water,
>   they became our bread.
>   But around our piety
>   night nothing said.
>
>   We travelled the roads,
>   struck by God's ire,
>   messengers we.
>   laved in fire.
>   Judgement, expiation,
>   the voice bade thus.
>   And the judgement came true,
>   but never the solace.
>
>   We sang in the fields
>   in rejoicing turned
>   towards new stars
>   that like symbols burned.
>   O dream, o hope,
>   how richly you flowed,
>   O promise's promise,
>   so deceitful and broad.

One prayer, one only
remains to us:
strike even harder,
you that cause pain to us!
Fold space together
and extinguish time,
annihilate all
and make peace come!

How long, how long, how long!
Destroy us!
Destroy us!

SOLO (*from* CHORUS I)
We know that the bitter fates
did not come to us first.
Who will say in suffering's flood:
ours is greatest!
Against times of plague and hunger's years
and the mothers' cry
in abandoned towns –
what do we weigh!

Oh, we were used to making
bolder demands,
but sensed that life gave us good
as a grace from its hands.
The dead know, they rest in peace,
how much the heart can thole. – – –
But we despair of man
and of man's goal.

We believed that by its own power
the truth won through.
But a stronger lure is lies'
inciting brew.
The drunken souls maim themselves
for the idol State,
and trust drowns in mistrust
and love in hate.

So we are the shreds that were wasted,
the hammer that broke.

Come, sweep your smithy empty and clean
with broom and rake!
Light the forge again to create
that which is not us!
A gleam was your spirit in man,
a gleam – and gone past.

CHORUS I
Destroy us!
Destroy us!

CHORUS II
A little time, a little time, a little time!
Have mercy!
Have mercy!

It must not end so
cruelly unreconciled.
Not so long as on earth still
life is spared.
Grant one more brief term
for the world's wheel to turn!
So dark the night persists,
perhaps a new one may burn.

If this seems presumptuous,
then forget all words
but let us be silent and endure our way,
like grass close to earth's swards.
Too deep the shame we saw,
too meaningless the agony.
On expectancy we lived –
waiting let us die!

Have mercy!
Have mercy!

SOLITARY VOICE (*from* CHORUS II)
Lord of the macrocosm,
lord of the microcosm,
you who burst all measures,
great and small,

you alone know
how measures and figures defraud,
you know that life is
what life always was.

He that walks over battlefields
and hears distress's cry,
the more he sees and hears,
grows his agony.
But there is no sum to be had
of the world's pains:
he merely slowly draws close
to what one soul contains.

The world's life is no sum,
but the way that souls tread,
no goal in sight,
but triumphs in shame clear-eyed.
You smile at our numbers and figures.
Let earth's purgatory go on burning!
Let us preserve all all
for the joy of overcoming!

CHORUS I (*dying away*)	CHORUS II (*dying away*)
Destroy us!	Have mercy!
Destroy us!	Have mercy!

Sloth

THE ACCUSER
    To you first, you who believe you are innocent,
    you slothful ones!
    A heavy burden you bind to yourselves,
    heavier than heinous crimes and heavier than the earth can bear.

    On you the guilt for all the evil that was not hindered!
    On you the guilt for all the good that was not done!
    A heavy burden! Because of you
    the world is going under.

CHORUS
> By our own hearts we were forsaken.
> Near their steep walls is our bed for the night.
> We are those doomed by life to a living death,
> thirsting in trance for the springs' water bright.
>
> Our arms we twine hard around our knees,
> stilled by tension and not by repose.
> Above the wall's crest float the fresh trees.
> Beneath their roots we hear the springs ooze.
>
> There are our lives. There are our souls.
> You who come to punish, what will you do to deliver us?
> If you know the way in, then all will be well.
> But if we leave the springs, the desert storm will shrivel us.
>
> Bring no pitchers to those hot, dry mouths!
> Never will we raise our hands for action,
> never – until we drink from the innermost wells.
> Near our hearts' walls we'll await transformation.

SOLO
> You cry out. Within me echoes
> an answer faint.
> but deep in all my valleys
> abhorrence remains.
>
> Someone there is, one solitary
> out of all my folk,
> willing to serve you, crier,
> to interpret, support.
>
> But see, I fear attack
> in the soul's world,
> the stupidity of the strong
> who conquer by the sword.
>
> Let my multiplicity slowly
> heal away,
> then perhaps one day each drop of blood
> may answer your cry!

How inconquerable would he be
in self-evident belief,
who could grow into one
in ripening peace.

How powerless from his living skin
would the day's dust fall.
How mighty in silence he would glide
from the great noise of it all.

CHORALE
All that is split and scattered
yearns to be healed and made better
and asks for faithfulness yet.
You live in our midst, around us.
Yea, though our doubting bound us,
Lord, you were hidden in it.

Lust

CHORUS
The daylight land is the alien land.
There we go clad in mask and armour.
There we go wrapped in name and past,
the cloaks of shame and the crowns of honour.
Here in the only and most extreme act
we shed the nine skins of the ego,
rise with closed eyes in the spring,
naked as foetuses and gods we go.
Naked as foetuses. The transfiguring night
beneath the human we touch, shivering,
follow in the tracks of primordial ancestors
deep sea dim and phosphorous-glimmering.

The millennias' copulatory hunger
devours and bears all earthly fate.
Human forms and names are transient
drops from the ecstasies' spate.

MAN'S VOICE

    Stunned, I awake – from what womb missed?
    What I perceived was no human tryst.
    I led a life on my self's sediments,
    and I was one of nature's elements.

WOMAN'S VOICE

    Darkness-blinded, in torpor I sank
    violated by phantoms, not by any man.
    They made me burn, the desires of earth's ghosts,
    and I gave birth to myth's monstrous hosts.

THE CHORUS (*continues*)

    Naked as gods. In formless dawn
    risen from the sea on the shore they stand.
    Without knowing their way and their realm
    they take one hesitant step across the sand.

    Without knowing what strength they possess
    they breathe gently, they stop and turn.
    The worlds awake from the touch of their breath,
    the depths and the heights flame alight and burn.

WOMAN'S VOICE

    How humbly immense a pride can be.
    I am a holy image, a symbol only,
    but translucent because a Power needs me.
    Your worship fills and far exceeds me.

MAN'S VOICE

    What became of our earthly being's weight?
    You reveal what life cannot yet create.
    I myself am fire. No one am I.
    Our realm deludes. Behind objects we lie.

THE CHORUS

    Do you mean to close the final way?
    Do you mean to dam the final spate,
    where our arid essence is watered by
    the worlds beyond all earthly fate?

Do you mean to choke in names all the nameless
timeless flame from the creative pyre
until the consuming miracle yields before
the will and the goal to which you aspire?

CHORALE
>O Lord, however you will judge us yet
>make us never forget
>how wide your kingdoms reach.
>In crowding here and dearth
>lust was, just like death,
>a sigh from depths that none can reach.

Pride

CHORUS
>How could you exist without us,
>you great, slow one.
>Where had you space to rise up from,
>if not in our pride begun.
>Your shelter and your rock-grave
>are here our hands, tight-wrenched.
>And hear, we pray, though not for mercy,
>with teeth together clenched:
>*I can bear it.*
>
>Around us clinging tough and blind
>are lives, swarming and riven.
>To man alone, highest and lowest,
>was empty despair given.
>In that which is made most wondrously
>there is much, too easy to blast.
>O bless our pride,
>that holds on to the last:
>*I can bear it.*
>
>What had we else, that would endure
>in lifeless wastes
>and solace dare itself create

from unreal mists –
from chaos compel form
born of burning homelessness,
give tones to tears and words to screams
and save itself in this:
I can bear it.

Here weighs a scale to give justice
to life and death.
How heavy it hangs, the cup of pain,
with our maimed fates.
How light the other, with all that is worth
our aspiration's call.
Put our holy pride in it, O Lord,
then gently it will fall.
I can bear it.

Conclusion

CHORUS
>Not even evil
>can you destroy,
>O heart of ours,
>but that you die,
>not one base demon
>to nothing lead,
>but that you smite yourself,
>eternal seed.
>
>Eternal seed.
>for none has seen you flower,
>only grow,
>always and many times over.
>All the way
>to meaning in all the void!
>Life's long yearning
>grant to us unalloyed.
>
>Grant to us unalloyed
>the day's heaviest hour,

its stifling agony,
for you are the morning star,
gleaming solace cool,
within the mist a spark,
borne on seven clouds,
seven dragons dark.

* * * *

A Form Am I

A form am I,
but my matter the primordial flame.
Fire is my gaze
and flames my hands.
In drunkenness that creates
twine the fire's tongues
insatiably around that play of lines
that is your being.

Form also you,
but form that is through-annealed,
etherized
raised from the depths' sea of fire –
mirage and image,
half-created and growing
– like all gods –
bubble above chaos.

Of all things
the gods are most transient,
of all things
worship is most enduring.
O bubble bubble,
moment and delusion
and through the fire
eternity's goal!

Odysseus at the Mast

Bind me, you warriors,
to the vessel's mast,
draw tight the ropes
secure and fast!
Commands nor prayers
shall none harken to.
Death's lure for me,
The wax for you.

Wax in your ears,
the oar in your hand –
no songs can reach you
from the dangers' land.
Until you are past and you
set me free again,
you have no chieftain
and I have no men.

King Agamemnon,
hope of Hellas' land,
steered, it is said – with mute sign
and earplugs firm rammed.
Ajax it is said did sail
near the monsters' call
boldly among his bold ones
towards ruin and fall.

They all are kings
for as long as they can.
None but I is a
lonely man.
Stronger than honour
and power and control
it lures me, the knowledge
I riskily stole.

It cannot be used
for every day's need,
it cannot be given away
cannot be bequeathed.
Bind me well, you warriors,
but leave my ears alone!
All that's heard, seen and felt
shall become my own.

Be Silent. Have Trust

In despair you cry:
Where is the wise word,
that alone will cure the world's
poisoned sores?
And where is the thought,
oh, give us the thought,
that leads out of time
where death's spirit soars!

Be silent. Have trust.
For our being is creation.
We are in a deep league
with that which wants to be.
Your great despair
Is not an empty dread
sometimes in the depths it has
a note of agony.

The blind dark suffers agonies
from secret dreams
that no one sees, and yet
they are near in all.
They cannot be told.
They cannot be thought.
They must first be lived through
to being and form.

Do not ask for words,
do not ask for thoughts,
but ask for a share in the agony
from our earth's root, interred.
The Silent is thinking
in flesh and blood and will,
and may at last hurl like fire
to you – its word.

The Trees

Alive like us
and far, far away,
so our word 'understand'
becomes empty smoke and wind.
Deeply inaccessible
to thought and sense,
though against our cheeks
your bark feels harshly kind.

Eyeless you shine
in delight and flowers.
Through what instruments
do you know your magnificence?
Through what secret,
creating knowledge
have you a share in the power
of visions and scents?

Leaning against the trunk
we are hardly noticed,
do not slip in to your
inner world's ring.
Or reach you, mirrored,
a scrap of our being,
to ourselves unknown
and frightening?

Though no doubt we were born
of the same ancestors,
not a glimpse of shared hours
our eyes have found.
Too many adventures
have divided us since,
too unknowable
is our simple ground.

Perhaps we still have
a tryst to expect,
on that road where life
is to soil returned.
Yet one more hand outstretched
between sundered kin.
And we thank death
because of that bond.

Our flesh, always borrowed,
we give it back.
Melt it down to your form,
and take and give!
Let it be exchanged between us
like friendly gifts,
deep beautiful unknown
sister life!

How Can Reliance Live?

Around us all is collapsing,
and more will collapse,
until no stone is left
to support our foot.
How can you still believe,
who have nothing to believe in?
How can reliance live
so lacking any root?

Is it itself a root?
Is it itself the seed?
and does the world's tree itself
grow out of it, then?
Then our fate is stored
in silent hearts.
Because of their silence
it may be day again.

Because of their wholeness
chaos may flower
from miracles' power – that is silent
but wants to be believed.
All things may be smashed asunder.
Again they may be healed,
as long as it is living,
our innermost seed.

Come, all that grows whole,
and transparently self-evident,
to us, we who reckon
and are on our guard,
and teach us that the day
we cease to reckon,
that is our lives' fulfilment
and our future power!

Christmas 1939

When Christmas Eve tautens
then floor and door creak.
Since times primordial the dead
as before us seek.
In our homes they take their seats
and us they remind
that in those ancient times
for them first Christmas was a feast.

'We come not with fear,
with comfort we come.
We saw your desertion
one dark autumn long.
How good to be with you in here.
Sit by the fire with us a while
We knew the horror, we as well,
it was like yours, our despair.

'We stood with frozen mouths
in the world's night at our post,
and the sky's congealed wells
lay ice-blue with frost.
Death's sting we came to know.
And death's snow lay wide.
Then someone said: 'Wait –
a morning star I saw.'

'We heard. We believed,
We lit torches in our distress.
And we rose up to the light-feast
in darkness and death.
You say: 'Fools' torches ablaze!'
And if you can, then douse them.
But lift them rather and hand them
from us to the new race!'
– – –

The empty winter skies
have smothered every cry.
But endlessly listen the souls,
the dead and we.
In some corner hidden away
by a world to destruction worn,
a child is being born,
a promised child on straw and hay.

Man's Multiplicity

Beautiful is a strong body,
that cleaves a hard wave,
Beautiful, beautiful is the child's sleep
after tension that playing gave.

Beautiful is the day of work
– hard bread, broken and blest –
and beautiful an hour that forgets in wine
the future and the past.

We were born of mothers of heaven and earth
and of powers with no end in view,
nocturnal wills and wills of light
with names that no one knew.

May one of the many
not gain power over us,
though she be of heaven's race
and shine in magnificence.

In us a multiplicity lives.
It fumbles towards unity.
Its capturing, gathering burning-glass
we were born to be.

Great is man's striving,
great the goals it has set –
but much greater is man himself
with roots in universal night.

So give, that we shield a secret room
and never a flame do lack
on the altar of an unknown god,
that may tomorrow wake.

We Who Do Not Dare to See

The few who dared to be
– blessed may they be! –
are maimed and slain all over again
by us who dare not see.

Darkened icons
of measure equal, all,
hang the images of the living, the burning,
cramped among much that is small.

The centuries have smoothed
their strange features away,
as we now zealously smooth
day after day.

We file and embellish
as best we can and may,
until nothing distinguishes spirit
from respectability.

The young go in search
of the fire that scorched.
They go with empty eyes
that have found nought.

They must suffer it all over again.
Poor ones, they!
We squandered the gain of the saints – we
who did not dare to see.

The Avenging Angel Speaks

Give me the dead part of your life.
I will be sure to wake it.
The nights await our pastime.
We will be sure to break it.
Though your day was so bloodlessly empty,
I can compel it to bleed,
compel it, in shame and judgement,
to rise up from the dead.

So, when day dawns and again you take hold,
you will see what you have gained,
you will see the mark of a living night
into your temple burned –
witness that that time you wanted to cheat
from mercy back you have got
and got it full to its flowing brim –
whether torment or joy, matters not.

They Stole Your Thought from You

They stole your thought from you? – You frighten me, blasphemer!
Who wants to own the mind is the mind's traitorous schemer!
Deep must the soul bow down to enter the kingdom's doors.
Perhaps you can become truth's – but truth can never be yours.

Drinking Sacrifice

Over rough red wine heavy foreheads bow.
It is not wine that weighs them down.
The wine that frees our thoughts the most,
it frees the least our tongue.

Like a secret blaze, sacrificial fire
is rough red wine.
I alone know before what powers
that smoke arises fine.

I alone know from what worlds
I fetch my drunkenness.
Each and all stare past the rest
and listen to distant sighs.

Each and all raise their glasses to things
that none of the others see,
in dark lands where rejoicing and grief
scarce have meaning finally.

So in secret I raise here my red wine,
my sacrificial blaze,
to a pain that is mine and resembles most
the eternal consuming gale from the seas.

Marsh Wanderer

Dark is my land.
Wanderer, who are you?
Marsh wanderer!
Blind lies my land.
Wanderer, who are you?
I feel footprints fill themselves
with blood from my inner self.

I would like to know your hands.
If they are of fire that burns,
let me feel it.
I would like to know your hands.
If they are like cool leaves,
then stroke them over the trees' pain
and let the dead awake.

The Flower Bitterness

Flower flower Bitterness,
how stand you now so full
of ripe gold honey
for all your bitter pall.
How sag you now with gifts,
the meadows' almond flower
the modest, gently swathed,
could surely never bear,

Torment and blessing –
each has his own.
I do not know life's measure,
but know that you became mine.
Your cup was like fire.
Your drink was like gall.
You offered seven sorrows,
and I drank them all.

Flower flower Bitterness,
how rich at last you grow
in heat-golden honey
resembling sunlight's flow.
Here, sated with sweetness,
I stand in your clear gift's rays.
I will rejoice with Adam.
With Job I will praise.

Never is the forest happy as now…

Never is the forest happy as now in sun and rain,
never so overflowing with delicate scents and glitter,
never so playfully consoling – only me it does not reach,
though I seek and pray. My pain is too bitter.

Drink, my eyes, gold candles I myself do not see.
Breathe deeply, my lungs, the wet moss's vapour.
I am a dead stone. Forget me, live for yourselves,
gather in golden chambers all that you can capture.

Inaccessible that room where day's harvest will ripen
soft with shimmers and scents and sighs. When the hour is nigh
a tautened splendour will burst its cell. Over me will pour
fresh and wild as a waterfall, pain's memory.

Wild Apple

How is it possible?
How did such a glorious multiplicity grow,
such a fresh and fine and airy cloud of flowers,
such a forest of twisted wild boughs,
such a rough bark with green lichen
all of it only

from one and the same dark small kernel?
There it lay, all of it,
trunk, branches, leaves and bark and airy flowers,
pressed together in a heart-shape.

But we are the wild apple's reflection in water.
From riches without boundary and bottom,
from young days' airy light fruit-blossom,
from a hundred roads' forest of clinging branches,
from the simple bark of a simple life,
we gather slowly,
until everything lies still, condensed, closed
within a heart-kernel...
How is it possible?

Now is the time of immense waiting

Now is the time of immense waiting
before the leafing time,
now the trees tremble in their bursting glory,
the birches in purple, the aspens in green
and in gold-red the willows of the streams –
time of invisible forces,
when all is only bearing wombs –
souls go pantingly heavy,
and the twilight excites and wearies
like unbridled trysts.
Now creation crouches, yearning's leap in store –
before disappointment comes,
when the forest is as green as possible
and the world is as complete as possible
the trees and the people mumble as in sleep:
'We wish for more.'

How can I say...

How can I say if thy voice is beautiful.
I only know that it pierces
and makes me tremble like a leaf
and tears me into rags and pieces.

What do I know of thy skin and thy limbs.
It only shakes me that they are thine,
so that for me there is no sleep or rest,
till they are mine.

To You

You my despair and my strength,
you took all the life I owned,
and because you demanded everything,
you gave back a thousandfold.

My poor young thing...

Afraid of the dark, my poor young thing,
who met spirits of another kind,
among the white-clad ever noticing
others of evil mind,
now I want to sing gentle songs to you,
they deliver from fear, cramp, coercion rude.
They do not ask that the evil should rue,
They do not ask for the fight of the good.

Then you shall know that all that lives
deep inside is of the same kind.
As trees and plants it can grow hesitantly,
by its own law upwards inclined.
And trees may be felled and flowers be broken
and branches die with their strength dried up,
but the dream hides itself – and wants to be woken –
in every living drop of sap.

You are the resurrection of my soul

You are the resurrection of my soul
to ecstasy in what is real,
so the air touches me hot as fire
like a sea of glass that I feel,
and the power of my eyes,
so that numbly they catch a glimmer
of how all the colours flame out
in a drunken shimmer.

You are the strength of my will,
you give me a fortitude
to wait and to act,
that I have never had,
Yes my senses' hunger,
that incite me and pursue,
becomes rejoicing every day
because it is for you.

You are my life's ripeness.
You make me whole.
Out of my past now gathers
each thread and smallest dole.
On a hundred different roads
I have walked and strived.
Now they meet. It is towards you
That I have lived.

Many voices speak

Many voices speak.
Yours like water calls.
Yours is like rain,
when through the night it falls.
Softly purls
in a fumbling dive,
slowly, hesitantly,
torturedly alive.

Trickles and strains.
trembling like a ground
against my skin,
behind every sound,
wraps itself softly,
closes me in,
fills my ears, whispering
memory's refrain.

I want to sit silent
where I cannot disturb you.
I want to dwell and live
where I can hear you.
Many voices speak.
Through them all
I hear only yours
like the night rain fall.

Your voice...

1

Your voice: in an old orchard a path half overgrown
with deep shadows and bright sun and birdsong sudden thrown,
a path of untamed secret life and breeze and loneliness –
how strangely lone and wild, it is only I who knows.

And when I wake at night, in it I waken then,
and I grow lost in green transparent shadow play again.
There I dwell for hours and hours and know that whom
you will follow and where you listen, here is my home.

2

Your voice: I have heard it for twenty years, and all that you have
            said
has lain submerged in me, but charged with power yet.
Now I hear it word for word as yesterday, it fills night and day.
It was the warmth of my veins. It was my heart, beating away.
What are these depths in us, where the past exists, all?
Or is it only your being, your voice that I recall?
You were my life's fulfilment. How has its ripening passed?
A choked tree, a tree of agony, burst into leaf at last.

3

All say it: your time is short, I know.
I cannot imagine that you will ever go.
There is no world to live in, where you do not live.
My mind denies the miracle. But in my heart, belief.

All things you contain...

All things you contain, more than a mortal can thole.
You are light and darkness in a double bowl.

How the one shimmers, naked and cool.
Mother-of-pearl air over water of opal pale.
Seeing, seen,
ready for day's gleam
dawns slowly open their mussel shell.

But dim and still does the other brood,
also a mussel, though deep where the sea is mute.
Not broken open,
since creation closed
it protects the mother-sleep's secret room.
All things you are, the whole of my being's goal.
You are the day and the night in a double bowl.

Linköping Cathedral
(February 1938)

I *The Altar Painting*

Do not seek here the silence of the dead.
The walls drip with the vigil of the ages.
The vaults tremble with living spirits
on their way back.
The centuries' ring
turns slowly around them.
All things are near. Past
is nothing.

The spirit that raised stone upon stone
like the driving sap of temple pillars,
has sprung a new bough.

From the images comes a flashing brilliance
of inexorable demand for sacrifice,
which our fathers heard and obeyed.
That man there with the narrow mouth
never sat happily by the evening well,
as the herds billowed wearily home
and a sorrow-dissolving twilight burned.
He is fire. The conflagration he bodes,
god as much as young man.
All that is secret he sees through
sternly as only the young can.
High in the bright arches of his purity
he offers war.
Over his forehead flame
Middle Ages, young and hard.

II

Centuries in kindred train,
prophet next to prophet,
darkly real against skies
of silver air and nothing.

So solitarily essential
in the phantom of creation,
man bears his heavy soul
as a stone in the epochs' cathedral. –

And their gaze is distant
among what does not die,
and their features are closed shrines
with frozen passion for a lock.

III

So heavily strikes the light
that no dust can bear it.
Go hence, light! You crush
the clay you take as dwelling.
How many have you visited
since primeval days –
and all all
prayed the same prayer: mercy!

How many have you wrestled with
and triumphed over
and consoled only with visions'
confusing promises.
How many went in the dawn
from the Jabbok's ford
with the sum of their life
in their maimed hips.

We saw their movements
of ugly deformity
and thought: Are they implements
for the light to use?
See, health's sunlight,
that gently cures the world,
is powerful in the healthy,
but these are sick. –

We saw their smile
and could not decipher it,
we saw their tracks,
which the legends relate.
Splendour of their heaven
and splendour of their hell
seized us like a drunkenness.
Who knows what he will choose?

Yes, who knows it still,
who knows the ways
that lead to the stone of the wise
and life's red kernels.
They risked their souls.
Then say, the Jabbok's mighty one,
have you a cure for the race
under the stars of the fear of death?

IV *The Tapestries*

But as the plants unfold
where the fields of late lay empty,
the earth awoke in space's spring
and slowly began to flower.

From fern forests and lizard slime
life crept up the precipice.
There a human child kneels
and looks out over the depths.

How did wings grow there in the birds' feathers?
How the chestnut's stick raised,
which carefully and proudly bore the finest candles
high above serpent and dragon?

We know of the spring, that the power of the depths
cannot have drained its source.
So let us perceive in all that is
the creating wellsprings' rising

and let go like Job on his torment's heap
of justice's tricks
and lean our sick and tough hope
against the miracle that is still a miracle.

Prologue at a School Prizegiving

There are courtyards and lawns that have rung so long
with cries and laughter and noisy games,
with shrill small voices and voices breaking,
that even in the solitude the stones echo.
There are rooms where the walls themselves have absorbed
so much raw healthy young life that it will never go,
and perhaps some yawns and perhaps some fear,
and perhaps some of the excitement that makes the hours too short –
and perhaps some of the times of endless listening
and perhaps some of the joy of discovery at old new wonders.
There are staircases that have been worn by generations of feet
in countless schools in countless lands
What a torrent has run between the school's walls
like a river rushing mightily between resting shores!

A river of young spring energy and new opportunities,
still seething with unrest and fermenting questions,
goes forth between banks which itself did not form,
with the future's seeds in its rumbling waves.
And the walls ask: Are we only the past?
Are we the obstacle that makes the energy break and be checked?
Is the inheritance we leave so overwhelming
that perhaps the future itself lets itself be dammed?
But then there is a murmur from trees and grass and rain:
That which is truly future, nothing can dam!
What we have gathered of experience, of dream and hope and will
is too costly to die when our lives are over.
We bore it to the river, the young, strong river,
which will perhaps take it towards the coming time.
And among all that we leave and all that it takes with us
there is much that will sink to the bottom and be forgotten,
but the best we found and the richest we lived
are the seeds that have energy and will be preserved and kept.

Thus in the great stream thought is bound to thought
and will to will, as the hours stride on,
until generation after generation let go of hands they held
and go to take up their task at last.
So they are bound here among games and lessons and dreams –
like links in the great community that stretches out seeking
towards all that we dare to hope –
the children of men to the whole of mankind.

Save the Children

Too clearly, frighteningly clearly
we hear the crack of the Spanish explosions.
Groaning in the wind, weeping in the rain
break the peace in silent evenings.
In the midst of self-satisfied states
people are forced to bitterly learn:
the earth has shrunk and become small;
never was the whole of Europe so near.

Out of the unending horizon
space closes tighter and tighter.
Soon now, when our children are grown,
there will be no more hiding-places or distances.
Full of anguish, with lips closed,
we wish luck on their future. – –
Children, whose eyes have drowned in horrors,
are growing to become their shadow and era.

Centuries of plague, times of pestilence
roll yet again across the lands.
Grant that we may at least endure
when it comes to the health of our spirits!
Terror and hate and the wild beast's foam
creep like plague-poison over minds.
He may be thankful, who was able to heal
some wound among his most grievous memories.

Roof over head, shelter from cold,
the bread that relieves naked need,
the warmth in the hand, the light in the voice –
these are weapons in the fight against death.
All is like circles around the stone: they spread
far out over the water's surfaces.
No one can know how far he will reach,
only that he fights on the side of life.

The Child

No worm, no seed in the wind
is armed more weakly against life's peril,
no baby bird is exposed
more helplessly to the mercy of the strong.
What daring of the hidden powers
to let themselves be born by human children
and pour the wine above all wines
into this bowl of thin temple-cork!

But in timid fear we approach
the eyes of the child, scarcely awake,
in which forms and colours are reflected
overwhelming, new, naked –
creators' eyes that will tame the visions
and slowly order the cosmos's home,
divide the waters from the vault above
and set earth's fastness between them.

And in fear and trembling we approach
those volcanic dawns
whose eruptions of fire and geysers
still rock us on slow swells:
then the day was deep and eternal,
strangely sated with a violent spring;
life burned intolerably,
like a sun in its blue years.

Remorsefully they draw near to us, near to us,
the sunken lands, thoughtlessly abandoned,
that hide our royal sceptres
and all that the Mothers intended as a miracle –
the earth's magic healings,
spiders' webs in morning dew,
and the sacred energy of growth –
all buried under the slag of the years.

Among the blind who seek power
in dead destruction,
the child walks like a sorrowless smile
of what makes alive.
On the day when the steel fails
and the peoples cry for the Primordial Flood –
on that day the child will have won,
on that day fate will change.

Those Quiet Footsteps Behind Me

If I listen, I can hear life flying
ever faster now –
Those quiet footsteps behind me –
death, it is you.

Before, you were far away –
I held you all too dear.
Now, when I long no more,
now you are there.

Dear death, there is in your being
something that comforts strife:
what do you care if one's grown great,
or wasted the whole of one's life?

Dear death. there is in your being
something that clears, makes pure:
all that's the same in the good and the bad
you lay open, naked and bare.

Follow me and let me hold your hand,
it calms one deep and well.
The beautiful you make indispensably great,
The ugly you make small.
It is as though you wanted something of me,
A present you want, I guess:
a strange, small curious key –
the little word 'yes'.

Yes, yes, I wanted!
Yes, yes, I will!
My piety I lay down at your feet
so life may grow more, still.

At the Bottom of Things

I read in the newspaper that someone had died, someone I knew
    by name.
She lived, like me, wrote books, like me, grew old, and now she is
    dead.

Think, to be dead and have left everything behind;
anguish, terror and loneliness, and the implacable guilt.

But a great justice lies hidden at the bottom of things.
We all have a grace to expect – a gift of which no one can rob us.

Where the divining-rod descends

Where the divining-rod descends
goes forth the water's vein.
a nodal point for fate,
a serious one.
Do not flee into dreams
of richer sward.
Here is your ground, and the powers
have said their word.

It may come to pass, if you dig here,
that the heather's mark
may be watered to a pleasure-garden
and leafy park.
It may also come to pass
that your toil will be repaid
with a few dark cracks
that wintergreen has made.

The one and the other
have meagre weight
against your touching your own fate's
living plate,
where evil power is broken,
where creation takes place,
where you and the world grow
to a greater space.

Do not think your dreams
will come true at last.
Do not think you will regain
those meadows you lost.
Where the divining-rod descends
stern mystery dwells below.
There happens nothing of what
you expect and know.

Take the shoe from your foot.
Be still, and watch the earth.
Here you are granted a tryst
with the power of birth.
How deep the earth ferments.
Her soul is like yours.
Here a way is opened for you
into hers.

Thus are we driven...

Thus are we driven, lost souls,
from camp-fire flame to camp-fire flame,
know nothing of our next rest
and nothing of the journey's aim –
know that night and day here alternate,
heavy evening and sunrise vast and strong,
and that our journey now seems short
and now too mercilessly long.

Yes, we know more: one sleepless night
in secret terror we silently hark
to our inner being, to a murmur
as of a subterranean brook
or of a shell's faint roar
in which the whole sea is yet heard,
and in our fear we cease
to ask which way we are led.

Thus are we driven, lost souls,
from camp-fire flame to camp-fire flame,
know nothing of our next rest
and nothing of the journey's aim,
but know that our hearts are drawn
inexorably, without choice
in towards the sea of an unknown home
that murmurs deep in the seashell's voice.

Those dark angels...

Those dark angels with blue flames
like flowers of fire in their black hair
know answers to strange blasphemous questions –
and perhaps they know where the bridge goes
from night's depths to daylight –
and perhaps they know the haven of all unity –
and perhaps in their father's house there is
a bright dwelling that has their name.

After Death

'What does it feel like when one grows wings, when one is dead,
         mother?'
'First your back bends, it grows broad and great.

Then it grows heavier and heavier. It is as if one carried a mountain.
There is a shaking and breaking in ribs and backbone and marrow.

Then it straightens up with a jerk and bears all, all.
Then one knows that one is dead now and lives in a new form.'

www.ingramcontent.com/pod-product-compliance
Lightning Source LLC
Chambersburg PA
CBHW021104080526
44587CB00010B/376